COOL
MEMORIES
V

COOL MEMORIES V

2000–2004

Jean Baudrillard

TRANSLATED BY CHRIS TURNER

polity

First published in French as *Cool Memories V* by Jean Baudrillard
© Éditions Galilée, 2005.

This English language translation copyright © Chris Turner 2006.

Polity Press
65 Bridge Street
Cambridge CB2 1UR, UK

Polity Press
350 Main Street
Malden, MA 02148, USA

ISBN-10: 0-7456-3659-4
ISBN-13: 978-07456-3659-7
ISBN-10: 0-7456-3660-8 (pb)
ISBN-13: 978-07456-3660-3

A catalogue record for this book is available from the British Library.

Typeset in 11 on 13 pt Sabon
by Servis Filmsetting Ltd, Manchester
Printed and bound in Great Britain by MPG Books Ltd, Bodmin

For further information on Polity, visit our website: www.polity.co.uk

And every god, similar in this to the God of gods Himself, is always bigger than the sphere of His action.

There is no point of equilibrium. Vibration alone produces the illusion of a steady balance, whereas everything runs to extremes on both sides.

Equilibrium exists only at the point of resolution of a zero-sum equation: death?

Never painted: I respect painting too much.
Never any politics: I respect power too much to take it.
Never any philosophy: I respect thought too much to traduce it.
Never made a claim to truth: I respect it too much to imperil it.
Never believed in reality: I respect it too much to believe in it.
Never had any imagining of death: it should remain a surprise.

There is an intoxication of all things, of good things and bad, of water and wine. But also a bingeing on all things – a bingeing on purity, on going one better, on sacrifice, all the more abject as it is the parody of intoxication.

The circumstances of your death set your conditions of existence in the afterlife forever. If you die unhappy, you will be so for eternity. If you die in an accident, you will relive it eternally.

If you die at the same time as your loved one, you will live eternally at their side. If you don't love them any more, what a dire fate.

In another mental constellation, can we imagine time becoming a sort of space in which you can move in all directions, return to the point of origin etc.? Conversely, could space become like time: irreversible, so that you can't retrace your steps or get back to the point you started from? Or having, like time, its absolute horizon: eternity?

What would be the equivalent of eternity where space is concerned? The negation of motion, stillness, or perpetual motion?

The woman juggling with cups and saucers.

All in all, it is such an acrobatic thing to do that you end up sensing the performance is rigged. But that doesn't detract in any way from the agility. It merely adds an ironic supplement to it.

I dream about a friend. Some time afterwards, I see him again in a dream and tell him I dreamt about him the other night. A dream memory recycled in a dream. Does this mean there's an alternative chain of circulation, from dream to dream and from one night to another?

Future generations of artificial beings will inevitably wipe out the human race, following the same impulse that led humans to wipe out animal species. They will see us retrospectively as apes and be ashamed of being descended from us. They will invent human zoos; protect us perhaps, like any endangered species, and make us the heroes of children's fictions.

The statistical rate of mortality means nothing. It is the rate of invisible mortality that counts. That is much higher, but incalculable, since death is here, growing everywhere and mounting up in the social body as a whole.

In the same way, there's no comparison between the index of visible corruption and that of invisible corruption (which it contributes to masking). The rate of political indifference is much higher than the abstention rate. As for the rate of invisible stupidity, it is far beyond the stupidity that actually shows up.

But perhaps the rate of secret intelligence and the rates of passion and imagination are also far higher than they appear?

The panic hole the Indians have: they dig holes, sit at the bottom and view the sky through the hole. An unrestricted view.

Our panic hole is the TV. Silence, blueness, clouds, birds, omens, weather – we have all that on the screen. We have the hole and the lid, the perfect niche.

When the hostage espouses the cause of the terrorist, the conqueror the cause of the vanquished, the torturer the cause of the victim, the master the cause of the slave – when contamination becomes universal in both directions, then another justice is active than the justice of the law, other scales than the scales of justice: at work here is an inalienable reversibility of all relations, even the most violently unequal.

Everything is mobile – water is mobile – air is mobile – blood circulates in the veins – time is relentless. Man alone is immobile.

For a healthy distribution of energies, the best thing is to commit one's cowardice to the service of a good cause and one's courage to the service of the bad ones.

The *Triumph of Death* fresco in the Palermo art gallery. Gruesome war-horse or baroque spectre . . . In fact, imagining death is impossible. You would need to be able to remember it.

Leucate. Same parish priest, same church. The great local innovation is Communion under the two species. If the faithful are reluctant to drink from the same chalice, God will not hold it against them. They can always dip their host in the priest's wine. All this new ritual passes over the heads of the general run of worshippers.

Homily on the Covenant struck with Moses, then sealed in the blood of Christ, and then in the Eucharist. Only Christ washes away spiritual stains. Silence falls.

There then enters a person who could well be the village whore – a blonde creature in a pale green miniskirt and with a boldly plunging neck-line. She slips quietly into the Lady Chapel, lights a candle for the Virgin Mary, then prostrates herself in prayer in a dark side-chapel before leaving again unseen. The Holy Covenant remains the one between the people of the village.

Any gloss on authors, their character traits or biographies, hides the fact that only bad writing has an author, good writing does not.

In the chapel at the seaside cemetery, all the votive offerings for the ship-wrecked that were stolen one day have been reproduced *a fresca* with astonishing perfection. What would happen if the originals were found again? How would it be with the copy of the real world if they rediscovered the original?

We have at this millennium end produced the perfect specimen of the species in the form of mobile-phone man. But even he will disappear before the future digital prosthesis, who will leave room in turn only for telepathic ghosts.

The events of a thousand years ago have shot off a thousand light years into space. Hiroshima is already sixty light years off. The moment that has just passed is already a light-second away. There is, then, no presence. Even if the discrepancy is infinitesimal, nothing is ever present – neither the wall nor the person opposite. We are barely even contemporaneous with our own existences.

Seen from a distant star, the monotony of current events takes on fantastic proportions.

Presumptuousness of the artist (John Cage, Bob Wilson?).

'We dream for those people who have no dreams of their own to keep them alive.' Always the same condescension – even worse when it relates to dreams and mental faculties. We may doubt whether the energy for dreaming among 'artists' or the vitality of the unconscious among the upper classes are any different from what they are among the common herd. There, at least, a kind of democracy prevails.

That an obscure Filipino computer-user can spread confusion through the global computer networks by launching the 'I love you' virus is possible only because the computer loves us and, feeling abandoned, like Hal in *2001: A Space Odyssey*, takes its revenge by suiciding the network.

Intelligence lies in deceleration. But you must first get ahead of things.

Doubtless science is, at bottom, merely a marvellous source of metaphors. The double arrow of time, the memory of water, apoptosis, black holes, anti-matter – where are we to find finer metaphors (let's give Sokal his due here)? And why not abuse them? They are the chrysalises of the concept.

One must believe in oneself, the world and reality only in homeopathic doses. A little superstition is all right, as is a little belief in reality – but only what is needed to cure evil with evil.

Fonda says to Nobody: 'Tell you what, first you get to be somebody and then you and me'll surround them'[1] (Which is a little bit like existence saying to him: first take the trouble to be born and you'll have the right to live.) He also tells him that when he has become Somebody, they'll 'make life harder and harder' for him and one day he'll be 'put down in history' by nobody. Nobody always wins out over Somebody. And, in fact, Nobody was quicker than him.

(*My Name is Nobody*, Sergio Leone.)[2]

The cow fed on bone meal, who ends up as a mad cow carcase and as organic fuel in the cement-works, the dust from which we eventually inhale.

Fire remains an ungovernable power and it is from fire that the most redoubtable vengeance will come: from sidereal fire and cold. All the natural elements were the chosen terrain of the gods. They will be the instruments of their vengeance.

Never lose sight of the fact that writing is a strange, inhuman function, a reflection of the inhumanity of language itself. Through writing, language, which is a domestic species, becomes a wild one again.

To integrate the end into the process: the only way of escaping mourning. To enjoy the end as a mirror magnifying the pleasure. One may even, in this sense, envisage integrating death as a magical factor.

Man has no definition; only the idea of man has one. Man can, then, have only an ideal definition of himself. Otherwise, what is there to say about him?

At the origin of misfortune, there is always an accident.
At the origin of good fortune, there is always a coincidence.

Around noon, a gathering darkness, as though it had welled up from the earth itself, not come down from the sky. As though produced by a source of black light, its beam sweeping across the earth at 2,000 kilometres per hour. The wind of the eclipse gets up in the gloom. It's the same silent wind as comes with storms. And cold descends from the solar corona. Path of totality.

'It sometimes happens that, through his mouth, words say true and profound things' (Schnitzler, *Aphorismen und Betrachtungen*).

It is aphorisms that best do justice to that cerebral electricity, those myriad microscopic ideas that ascend from the nerves to the brain and are constantly passing across it. They bear witness to that Brownian, corpuscular activity 'beyond the lenses, beyond the frosted glass', as Lichtenberg would say.

We dream mindlessly of the facts of the day. I read the story of a woman who kills herself by jumping from a train window. That night I have the same dream, slightly transposed. It would have been so much more original to have the dream and find the self-same story reported in the next morning's papers.

It is because of alterity, otherness, that no one can make himself laugh by tickling himself.

Just as there is no 'objective' existence of the sky's blueness (blue is blue and that's all there is to it), so there is nothing objectively knowable about the movements of the soul. They can only be intuited: psychological azure.

Those women who electrify you mentally (not necessarily physically), to whom you cannot speak cool-headedly and who put you in a state of having to please them.

Do not take the side of those already in the right.

Barthes: language is fascistic, since it perpetually commands us to speak. Phatic function, fascist function. The fanaticism of the signifier (Ferlosio). The German language was destroyed at the same time as the German cities (Sloterdijk).

Our sense of existence is a plate photosensitive to black light. It is made up of self-hatred and its immediate reparation.

Instead of dreams being the place where desires from real life are fulfilled, it would be the real that was the place where desires born of dreams would be fulfilled.

Dreams would be a search engine. The Aborigines, for example, scorning biological paternity, give priority to begetting by dreams. Reality would gain by this in becoming much more mysterious and dreams would cease to be the dumping ground of the unconscious.

It is immoral to keep beauty in the register of the sublime alone and not to find an equivalent for it in a charitable undertaking.

In the same way as the mentally handicapped will be entitled to damages for the fact of being born, every citizen should be able to claim a natural right to intelligence and therefore, in the worst of cases, demand a stupidity support allowance. The most difficult thing will be to assemble the evidence.

Death orders matters well, since the very fact of your absence makes the world distinctly less worthy of being lived in.

Exactly like the shaft of wit, the character trait or facial features, the fragment is made up of contradictory lineaments of meaning and their happy coincidence. The aphorism is like the starry sky, the blanks in it being the intersidereal void.

We should invent days without afternoons, nights that stop before the dawn, seasons that overlap at a quicker and quicker pace, a year that ends before beginning, and an endless alternation of joy and adversity.

Thus, with the sardonic collusion of diverse, but often baleful constellations, the philosophical subject emerged into the ultraviolet spectrum.

What is exceptional hardly deserves to live. What is banal does not even deserve to die. He was so banal that he didn't even deserve to be called Bernard.

Behind its generous appearance, the famous Warhol 'fifteen minutes of fame' is in fact contemptuous – an assignment to promotional mediocrity. And moreover, as the stock of 'fame' is limited, just like the stock of eggs in the uterus, it is supremely anti-democratic. If you are famous for a whole hour, you thwart three other people, who were entitled to their fifteen minutes.

Everything is becoming functional. Irony is disappearing in the critical function, the word is disappearing in its phatic function. Worse: critique, ethics, aesthetics become functions of each other, as they wait to become useless functions.

The master-thinkers of the democratic cause would be very surprised to learn that the people themselves are driven, at the deepest level, by the aristocratic principle. Even if their 'real' demand is for equality, liberty and material well-being, the spiritual wellspring of popular aspirations, the obscure object of their desire, remains fame, fortune and sacrifice.

The best thing would perhaps be to remove consciousness surgically *in utero*, together with irony, criticism and intelligence – all those qualities that are so fragile and so dangerous to existence in general. One might take advantage of this (all in a specialized Psycho-Genetic Institute, akin to the Institute of Zodiacal Semiurgy, where the surgical removal of star signs is practised) to be rid of the Unconscious, the extraction of which, like the extraction of all the irregularities of the genome, would be a great relief for future generations.

Theory is never so fine as when it takes the form of a fiction or a fable.

The story (by Amélie Nothomb) of the young woman who lives as a recluse, in the belief she is disfigured. Every possible means of seeing herself has been taken from her – no mirror, no reflections, not even a reflection from mercury in thermometers. Twin sister to the Duchess of Palagonia whom the Duke had surrounded with distorting mirrors which made her look monstrous and dissuaded her from becoming proud. This sequestration of beauty, this violence done to the right to see oneself, *il sacrificio della bellezza* is not just the problem of the peril women represent for men, it is also the problem of the danger posed to women by their own appearance.

A statistic tells us that the danger of a fatal air accident is one in 1,600,000. If you travel by plane every day, you are not in danger of crashing until a thousand years from now. The figures are meant to be reassuring, but in fact they are a source of horror since, by underlining the fact that the risk is real, though infinitesimal, they cut across the imaginary gamble we each make, which is the gamble on zero risk – without which we wouldn't take the plane. The thousand years become a finite horizon, the horizon of death, which moves closer as soon as we leave pure chance behind to enter the realm of probability.

The answerphone that stops as soon as you stop speaking, or speak too slowly. Closedown for reasons of silence!

Recovering some secrecy, some silence, some distance . . .
Recovering some conflict, some prohibition, some spectacle and violence . . .
Recovering the joy of the fully fledged spectator.

Freedom, will, responsibility – to sweep away all these categories, as it was necessary to sweep away those of soul, sin, immortality and the concepts of heaven and hell to deliver ourselves from the religious and the feudal.

To speak of death, you have to be alive. The living person has more chance of having an idea of death than the one who is already dead. In the same way, one doubtless has to be a man to speak about women. A man has more chance of having an idea of woman than a woman, who already is one.

At any rate, men certainly retain a memory of the woman they were in another life. In this way, they can have a finer intuition of her, filtered by multiple states of consciousness.

Why fight endlessly for a cause? Has anyone ever fought for the effects?

Getting used to the idea that the world is an effect without a cause, or in which the effect precedes the cause. Our actions themselves precede us and, one thing leading to another, are governed by the same paradox. 'A person's actions . . . are commonly continuations of his own inner constitution . . . [in] the way the magnet bestows form and order on iron filings.' (G. C. Lichtenberg).[3]

There is reason to be jealous at being seen by others from the outside and having only that distorting mirror of oneself that is self-knowledge.

The world as singularity resists the global as idea. Woman resists the idea of woman. Any confusion with one's own concept produces a lethal haemorrhage.

It is almost normal to lead a double life when you are alone. It is much more difficult when there are two of you.

At last, a genuine madman in the street – someone who doesn't need a mobile phone to talk to himself.

Some encounters stay in the memory thanks to the tone of voice, which you remember on an infra-red scale, so to speak, without being able to pinpoint it.

A woman's body and her face are quite distinct things. And one can, between the one and the other, descend from pure contemplation to pure concupiscence. Seen close up in love-making, the beauty or ugliness of the face disappears – carnal desire scorns distinctive features; it even overlooks differences of body and gesture to a very large extent. But desire is only rarely carnal, and sometimes it attaches to the facial features alone.

The worst thing is not so much being regarded as an impostor, but being regarded as a harmful object, a nuisance, by these high-flying vermin.

Beyond the end: the ideal non-place.
'In the very midst of the event, of the seduction, he was already at the memory of it – deep down, he was already finished with it' (Kierkegaard).

Beyond the end: the only unrestricted view.

Running after your shadow: the only way out from perpetual motion.

Dispersing the viewpoints: the only solution to the squaring of the circle.

His hypocritical air derived from the fact that he suffered simultaneously from an inferiority and a superiority complex towards himself.

The principle of insufficient reason: the only things that really take place are those which do not have sufficient reason to do so.

'Man is so sensitive to perfection that reason can make him an idiot.' (Lichtenberg).

The condemnation of sects is, like any witch-hunt, disgraceful: 'mental deficiency', 'cult of the guru', 'suicidal drive' etc. As though all these things were not standard in the normal sphere of conventions and the social order. This is reminiscent of the charge of 'cowardice' made against suicides.

Stalin's double. Since he wasn't a perfect likeness, they touched him up using plastic surgery, after which they eliminated all his relatives and all the witnesses to the operation. He played his role so well that in the end he came to think he was Stalin (as did Stalin himself!). At that point they sent him to the Gulag. But so well did he identify with his role that, on learning of Stalin's death, he died three days later.

The proof of how poorly grounded freedom is is that depriving someone of their freedom itself no longer means anything. Impossible to find an equivalence between the crime and the punishment or, therefore, any possible 'justice'. Given the extension of responsibility and its ramification into all networks, the irresponsibility is the same everywhere.

All these novels in which the authors try desperately to dramatize their own histories, their experiences, to recount their own psychological dramas – this is not literature. It is secretion, just like bile, sweat or tears – and, sometimes even, excretion. It is the literary transcription of 'reality television'. It is all the product of a vulgar unconscious not unlike a small intestine, around which roam the phantasms and affects of those who, now they've been persuaded they have an inner life, don't know what to do with it.

Paedophilia: the very term is disgusting. It is one of those words by which language takes its revenge, by which the thing denounced avenges itself on the denouncers.

The striptease artiste becomes seductive when she closes her eyes to her own body, blotting out those looking at her and being visible now to herself only from the inside. She comes closer at that point to her role as pure object, the secret of which she keeps to herself.

Whether you work by will or by chance, there are always as many fortunate and unfortunate coincidences.

Concordance between a 'real' situation and a discourse ought to be an indication of 'truth', but it is, for that very reason, philosophically unbearable.

The fragment is like a broken mirror – ideas don't have the time to reflect themselves in it or, as a result, to feel sorry for themselves. They run ahead of their shadows or their reflections.

To run ahead is to move towards an unforeseeable outcome, but one whose path is made for it in advance. Birds too run ahead of those who see them. The event also runs ahead of history. It is what opens up untimely perspectives in a world brought totally up to date.

To move in the space of deafness is like moving in an aquatic milieu. The same foetal, amniotic strangeness, the same cautiousness of gesture, the same mental lethargy – the same silence of the depths: it isn't you who are deaf, it's the world that's dumb. But the inner noise, the organic murmur is there. The body is all ears towards the inside.

Dart a very fine reed into the victim's heart. He will be left with a lethal stupefaction, but will not die of it. Dart a very fine glance into the eye of the torturer. He will be left with eternal remorse, without even remembering it.

'May he who speaks of himself never tell the whole truth, may he keep it secret and yield up only fragments of it.' This is the principle of 'scrupulous delicacy' according to Kierkegaard. Could one not also speak of a 'scrupulous violence' or an 'unscrupulous delicacy'? This rule of scrupulous fragmentation applies equally in analysis and writing.

Thought is that invisible blade that determines the separation of bodies.

The truth that sees itself as such becomes a lie and a deception, but language, which never lies, wins out over both.

The obsessive impression of having missed something – a (profound or insignificant) idea that has managed to pass unnoticed, a fundamental hypothesis that has slipped away, wound itself up like a curled snake in one's mental space and could only come out by unwinding itself the other way. Perhaps it is hidden deep in some previous life, perhaps it is part of a future life.

It is the secret continuation of the Nothing in the heart of things that creates the impression of having missed the crucial point.

The speed of transfusion that applies to effects liberated from their causes is viral. Any cell, any organ whatever, becomes viral as soon as it is no longer subject to the sovereign legislation of the whole body. Hence a new pathology beyond the organic, even beyond the psychosomatic, which is still linked to the individualization of the 'soul' and the body.

No mechanic now for modern cars, no doctor now for modern pathologies. The infinitesimal calculus of viral pathologies, unlocatable by traditional diagnostics, has entirely outstripped the mechanics of the body, just as the electronics of the modern car have outstripped the knowledge of its user. But one can imagine an electronic 'smartness' of the body (like 'smart' cars or houses) that would inform you of all its anomalies, or even, by a kind of GPS effect, of your position in the space of human relations.

All effects are perverse in so far as they run free of their causes: epilepsy of reality. The very possibility of effects without causes, or causes without effects, or effects producing their causes in a retrospective sequence, destabilizes any logical order and leads into a paradoxical one.

Admiration: a real sacred prostitution in which the most alienated is not the one you think. Thinking in these terms of a gentle violation, Lichtenberg spoke of a 'virginity of admiration'. And of those who remain virgins all their lives.

It is where there is the most violent contrast and where reconciliation seems impossible that seductiveness is at its most profound.

Illusion is the most obvious of things, the obviousness of the tangible appearance. Reality, for its part, is merely a flag of convenience.

The coalition of all those who find the mere hypothesis of a mystification or machination of any kind where reality is concerned unacceptable from the moral standpoint: the conspiracy of imbeciles.

A constant trumping of hypotheses in all disciplines, linked to the fierce rivalry between scientists. And, above and beyond their rivalry, to their solidarity on a single point: if truth were established definitively, that would put an end to science and the scientific community. Now, the survival of that community takes precedence over the survival of objective knowledge. And this is a vital reaction. It means that rival passions will always win out over the establishment of a final truth. That 'truth' will always be shot through with some passion from elsewhere. Paradoxically, the scientists apply themselves to this by producing ever more hypotheses. But the world itself systematically sidesteps truth. In the end, there is after all collusion between the scientists and their object, but collusion of an unexpected kind: in the art of escaping truth.

In its excess, information merely adds to the sum of useless knowledge and thereby swallows up communication, which in turn, by its infinite ramifications and the sum of superfluous exchanges, swallows up information. Things are the same in the media space as they are in the physical space of molecules: the same progressive dilution – and even vanishing – of substance as in the memory of water.

The 'disocculted' pataphysicians seem as though they have been defrosted. They look as if they have aged artificially in an aquarium. Perhaps it would have been preferable to stay occult?[4]

Only one thing is more useless than the refined playing of the hotel pianist and that is the air hostess's demonstration of how to use a lifejacket.

The eighth wonder of the world is in New Zealand, but it is forever invisible. The translucent cataract of gypsum and crystals produced by the age-old, subterranean action of geysers, the opalescent extravaganza that swept down into the lake, was smashed to smithereens and buried when the mountain split apart on 10 June 1886. Jealous nature has hidden it from our gaze, as though it wanted to save it from becoming a world heritage site.

Taking a plane which is so quick that you can see the sun rise in the west. Moving quicker than the daylight to lose yourself, from east to west, in the preceding night. But we are too slow and the darkness remains out of reach. When you see the sun rise from a plane, it is still darkest night on the ground. When it sets, night has already fallen on the ground – it is always lighter at altitude. You can never be in darkness at altitude and have daylight on the ground. Anyway, at 10,000 metres, neither night nor day rises or sets. You enter them like a projectile, with all the speed of the aeroplane.

Sublimation: the direct transition from the solid to the gaseous state (the ice evaporating on the Saint Lawrence). Sublimation of the phenomenal world: this subtle, volatile quality of substances, forms and colours.

Against Machiavelli's *Prince*, a treatise on the ploys of domination, we should set a treatise on the ruses of servitude. Its ploys are not those of the lion, but of the fox; not those of the eagle, but of the moray eel and the chameleon.

Arrogance is a head-on thing, but contempt is reptilian. And it paralyses its victims imperceptibly. This is what happened with Mitterrand in his relations with his followers and courtiers. And this is what brought him retrospective contempt, for one can respond to contempt only with equal contempt or death.

This blind constancy of trees and the plant world in producing leaves and flowers as the cycle ordains, out of pure vegetal instinct. In the animal kingdom too, faithfulness to the species is almost immutable. What would be the equivalent of this constancy in human beings? Might it be the blind determination to behave as a human being in the most inhuman conditions? Or the opposite: the determination to choose evil, including one's own misfortune, when all the conditions are ideal? Man's inexhaustible genius in reviving what is likely to annihilate him. There is no doubt that, as Mishima says, man turns the very difficulty of bearing his existence into a weapon.

As in the loose conglomeration of genes and molecules, where the proteins govern each other without it being possible to pinpoint the prime mover, so in the loose conglomeration of categories that govern our actions, everything is similarly interconnected: being able, willing, knowing, believing, having-to, etc. In order to be able, one has to wish to, and in order to wish to, one has to be able. And to know, one has to be able to know, and for that one has to wish to. And one further has to believe . . . etc. etc. To live simply, we have to break up this sequence: to split off willing from being able, to split off believing from knowing, to split off having-to from acting, to split off being from having-to-be.

The truth they defend is merely the astrological sign of their stupidity.

The satrap is a being who exercises no function, occupies no role, and acts by his mere presence – or by his absence, if he is transcendental.[5]

With the heat of summer comes the return of that hieroglyph more mysterious than the circulation of the blood or of commodities: the stochastic, zigzag flight of the fly in the middle of the room, beneath the central light fitting or in the sun's rays.

As flat as the earth before they noticed it was round. As ambiguous as the truth before they noticed it was true. As real as reality before they noticed it didn't exist. As beautiful as a woman before they noticed she wasn't one.

And is the earth really round? It is when seen from another world. Just as the real is real only from our phenomenal point of view. Or, rather, from the viewpoint of the unverifiable hypothesis of its non-existence.

'If the people will not obey the watchwords of the Revolution, then we must change the people' (Brecht). If the real refuses to conform to objective knowledge, then we must liquidate the real . . . 'If the truth hurts, it is the truth's fault.'

The Turkish political prisoners let themselves die of hunger rather than be transferred from their collective cells into individual ones: isolation is worse than death.

The time when perfection was of the order of crime is over, when beneath perfect beauty something criminal lay hidden. With the cloning and recycling of the species in conformity with an ideal norm, it will no longer even be a crime to be perfect. The exactitude of the creature will shine in the genetic firmament. There will be a universal presumption of innocence and a total excommunication of evil. This technical redemption of all the taints of the species will render any new divine intervention useless. There will no longer be any Last Judgement.

Reality for us is a little like the ground for trapeze artists, who work with a net without knowing that beneath it the ground has disappeared.

In this way, screens allowed the real to slip away. In this way, icons allowed God to slip quietly away.

He is writing the day-by-day account of his life, from the beginning. The first ten notebooks have brought him to the age of fifteen, during the war. At this rate it will take him twenty years to get to the current period. In the meanwhile, he will have grown old – the two parallel lines, that of the life and that of the narrative, will never meet. But it is also a wager, since in a way it wouldn't be right for the life to stop before the narrative catches up.

When God created man, He saw that he couldn't survive in that solitude and gave him a shadow. But since then man has never stopped selling it to the devil.

I knew him in all conditions. Moist in sacrifice, hostile or welcoming, voracious or retractile, excited or indifferent, impulsive and without qualms, dreamy on his best days.

That people who share the same genes should be separated by a moral chasm helps us to reassess the values in the name of which they are killing each other.

What is one to do against an enemy whose weapons are conformism and stupidity? Should one make oneself more conformist and more stupid? If his strategy lies in cunning and achievement, should one make oneself more cunning, more of an achiever? Should one make oneself more mediatic than the media?

War is impossible, and yet it takes place. But the fact that it takes place in no way detracts from its impossibility. The system is absurd and yet it functions. But the fact that it functions in no way detracts from its absurdity. The fact that the real exists in no way detracts from its unreality.

Image indicates the venal value of the man who has lost his name, just as transparency is the quality of the man who has lost his shadow.

L. D., speaking of the faces he photographs incognito in the metro:
'They are anonymous, I make them exist.' Exist yes, but how?
One of them stated that the hardest thing was to realize, when faced with his own photo, that he was nothing, nobody. Nothing but a captive face for a hidden lens.
The photographer, by contrast, is not anonymous. He claims to eclipse himself in the operation, but what he manages to eclipse is his relation to the other, *l'autre* (which is, paradoxically, the title of the book and the exhibition).[6]
So, all this aesthetics is merely a subterfuge: the more the contemporary artist plays with the nothing, the more his signature is fetishized.

Today things travel faster from Paris to Rio than from the hand to the brain. You have only to think of a friend at the other end of the world to be connected to him in real time. There is something inhuman in this instantaneity. I didn't necessarily want to be immediately in contact with him. I just wanted, perhaps, to toy with the idea of seeing him.

Boredom is out of luck: it is itself being discussed in crashingly boring terms.

'In the daytime I don't see. So I don't want what I don't see. Night is the tricky time, since at night, when I'm asleep, I see. I see streets, lights, a person dear to me. All in all, when I'm asleep, I act as though I were awake, and when I wake up, I act as though I were asleep' (E. de Lucca).
Do the blind see in their dreams?
To dream without seeing is even stranger than a waking dream, since dreams, for us, are primarily images – almost a film. It seems to us that dreams can do without images even less than reality can.

The profoundly negationist character of information, the demand for which has no concern for any historical reality or any moral meaning. Shoah or no Shoah, if Hitler were alive he would be on all the screens.

Might Network Man be the model for the disabled person of the future? It is perhaps to him, rather than to the paralytic, that we shall have forcibly to restore the use of his body.

An illness that breaks out opportunely just before the departure date and ends exactly on the day the trip was scheduled to end.

Memento mori: Not: remember that you must die, but: don't forget to die, remember to die (before it's too late).

Their faces are close to each other in sleep, but their dreams are light years apart. Their breathing mingles, but their thoughts diverge far beyond their bodies.

One's closest friends are a bit like the bad conscience of what you have become, and in their eyes your life becomes a vaguely criminal matter, something of a slow-motion murder.

Just as dust is what is born out of the erosion of all landscapes, so the real is what remains from the wearing down of all systems.

Further and further towards perfect resemblance. The voice of the airport announcer and integral music. Tomorrow's Eve.

'History is speeding up? No: history has stopped, but it has left us with the acceleration' (Philippe Muray).
The Judgement of God? No: God is dead, but He has left us his (last) judgement.

The Cheshire Cat has vanished, but he has left behind his smile.

The reality principle has disappeared, but it has left us with reality, which keeps on running like a headless chicken.

Artificial intelligence? The intelligence has left it, but we are left with the artifice, which flourishes the better on the ruins of intelligence.

Rights, if not desires, are left to us by things that take their leave. Transparency, as it removes itself from the scene, leaves us the right to see it clearly. Life, in withdrawing, leaves us the right to live. Everything, as it distances itself, leaves us the possibility of conceiving it.

We shall never know whether thought is an imposture, and that is providential.

'The people is, in some cases, so enlightened that it is no longer indifferent to anything' (Montesquieu). That is indeed the end point: when there is no longer anything about which there is nothing to say.

Verdict of a Chinese writer on a monstrous tree that is at once a blackberry and a bamboo: 'any disorder appearing in nature is the sign of a hidden disorder in the administration of the Empire . . . Order restored in nature clearly indicates satisfaction in heaven.' Our current blossoming of monsters and clones, hybrids and chimeras, our systematic mixing of mores and cultures, sexes and genes, cannot but attest to an irremediable disorder in the highest spheres of the Empire.

For an architecture to have a reason to exist, that is to say, for it not to arouse, even in the imagination, the desire to destroy it, it has to know, itself, how to convey a sense of the void, and a transparency other than that of glass.

First victim of the screen: silence. No living silence on television ever again, but minutes of artificial silence, of dead silence, stocked like spare parts or replacement organs, for the needs of the programme. The recording of the artificial silence is the ghostliest, most ludicrous operation I've ever witnessed.

Propitious or ill-fated, there is an exaltation in the fact of something happening to you. The fateful always wins out over the evaluation of good and bad.

Hugo describes perfectly the profile of the end of History: 'The twentieth century will be happy, there will be no more events.' And it is true, there are fewer and fewer. But historical experience has been replaced by an almost millenarian obsession with the Eventful, the Accidental and the Unforeseeable. We are almost back to the times when the hope was still alive of witnessing the coming of the Kingdom of God 'in real time'. Except that the expectation now is, rather, of the end in real time.

It seems that, after a long period of primitive accumulation, science has now lost any illusions as to its final ends, and is given over to the craziest hypotheses – free of any verification. It then sometimes recaptures the charm of the ancient cosmogonies.

The Stockholm Syndrome, the Theatre of Cruelty, voluntary servitude, living coin, the ready made, the accursed share, the total social fact, dust-breeding, the perfect crime – we find all these figures in the reality-TV cocktail, in that potlatch of vacuousness. It even drags the judgement that condemns it into its vacuousness.

C. M. wishes to be done with the artificial mystery of seduction. She wishes to overcome desire by wearing out pleasure. But pleasure is not like freedom, which Lichtenberg said was best used by being abused. She herself says she wants to be like a spider in the centre of her web. She has forgotten that it is the web which, intangibly, imperceptibly, weaves its spider.

Time was when virtual creatures emerged from the Unconscious. Today they are the products of digital calculation. We are no longer the theatre of their imagining. The oneiric function disappears in the expurgated screen version, much as, with language, only the phatic function survives or, with the gaze, only the scopic function remains.

The sphere of ideas is a jungle, a nature red in tooth and claw in which the natives are condemned to hunting and self-reliance. No heritage, no references, no primitive accumulation: thought has luck alone on its side, and instinctive, animal defence. So far as our conditions of life are concerned, we have become stockbreeders and producers. But mentally and affectively we have remained hunters. At every moment, in thought and writing, there is a prey and a predator. And survival is a miracle.

The extreme of happiness leaves room for only one question: might we not already be dead?

In the gorges, there is no ideal viewpoint. From below you don't get the idea of depth. From above, you can merely contemplate them abstractly, having only an aerial view. Only the birds have a total, side-on perspective.

What they contemplate, what they prostrate themselves before all along the beaches is their own sunset. If their existences could be diffracted in this way into the volcanic dusts, if their heads could be set ablaze with a fine coral dust, if their bodies could cross the horizon, the limit of which retreats as life nears its end, like that of the silence or fury of events, if one could rise up vertically so that the line of the horizon becomes first a curve, then a sphere, then an immaterial point relieved of any surface and depth . . .

'*Aphorizein*' (from which we get the word 'aphorism') means to retreat to such a distance that a horizon of thought is formed which never again closes on itself.

The lizard is the sprightliest animal and at the same time the closest to absolute stillness, darting as it does between the stones like a shaft of wit. Close, too, on the wall, and equally still in an entirely different universe, the hairy spider in its hexagonal web.

Chance does not exist. Either the universe obeys objective laws or it is of the order of will. But not of a will like our own: an inhuman will, in which all beings, minerals, animals, stars and elements are endowed with effective determination. Where the effect is an added extra, regardless of the cause, where the event is an added extra, regardless of history – chance being merely the intersection of all these wills. A universe consisting of antagonistic impulses, in which everything is lucky or ill-fated – isn't that more uplifting than the mere preoccupation with causes and consequences?

The downplaying of reality is a philosophical intuition and there is, therefore, nothing 'negationist' about it. The virtual, in its project of liquidating the real *technically*, is truly negationist.

Just as repressed sexuality has taken its revenge in the total hegemony of the sexual (which no longer has anything to do with sex), so repressed illusion takes its revenge on reality through the virtual (which no longer has anything to do with illusion).

Black faces are like basaltic lava emerging, against the sunlight, from the entrails of the earth, like black, light-absorbent mineral. The photographic film cannot capture them.

A woman may have all the marks of being a woman and yet not be one. The sex itself is not enough – it takes femininity to make a woman.

'It is not true that the unconscious goal in the evolution of every conscious being (animal, man, mankind, etc.) is its "highest happiness": the case, on the contrary, is that every stage of evolution possesses a special and incomparable happiness neither higher nor lower but simply its own' (Nietzsche).[7]

Language – any language – has a fine ring to it when it has no meaning (in magic, it is, in fact, this meaningless language that exerts its charm on material things). As soon as it means something, language merely peddles the banality of the common speech of all languages the world over.

In this country, the towns and villages are not a refuge from the desert, they give the desert sanctuary. They do not fortify themselves against it, they weave it into the houses or the inner courtyards, where the dusting of sand is the same, in the spaces of beaten earth where camels, donkeys, children and women mingle freely. Space is never under house arrest here. Shouldn't all architecture be inspired by the void and make it circulate in this way, instead of exiling it to a now captive urban space? We shouldn't have to travel through space, it ought to travel through us, the way Chuang Tzu's butcher's knife cuts through the interstices of the animal's body.

'Humanity will not be able to conceive itself as such until it encounters another conscious species . . .' There is a great presumptuousness in wishing to measure oneself against some other species only on the basis of consciousness. That is a distorting mirror which prevents us from seeing that the confrontation already exists outside of consciousness, in the infra-human, in the animal, in the unfolding of the world without us, outside of us. No need for an extra-terrestrial species for that: otherness is there, and it is everywhere a challenge to consciousness as it conceives itself hegemonically and as sole judge of the existence of the world.

It is possible that the human species hopes, by way of artificial intelligence, to invent another race, in which it can be reflected, as in an immense mirror. But, in reflecting itself, all it would be doing is verifying its existence. Now, consciousness is sufficient for knowing oneself, but it is not sufficient for conceiving oneself. For that, we have to be challenged in our very consciousness by all that does not enjoy this 'higher' consciousness, but which nonetheless, in the order of the world, is the equal of consciousness. Consciousness is sovereign only in the terms of the representation of the world it imposes, and imposes on itself. In the symbolic order, it can only measure itself against something bigger.

Regarding Stockhausen's declaration on the destruction of the Twin Towers as the finest work of art of modern times, why does it have to be a 'work of art'? Why must the sanction for the sublime and the exceptional always come from art? It's a scandalous misconception to attach the same high-class label of 'art' and performance to September 11th and the Palais de Tokyo, for example. Let us retain for events the power of the event.

'There are too many Jews on the France Culture radio station,' says Renaud Camus, and he is accused of racism. But the problem lies elsewhere and goes far beyond the Jewish question. It is, more generally, that there is too much of everything everywhere. Too many people, too many places, too many images on television, 'too many notes in Mozart', too many ideas and too many words to express them – too many old people among the old, too many young people among the young. And, ultimately, the worst of it is that there's too much culture on France Culture.

Marxism, Christianity and psychoanalysis have found refuge in Latin America. God, the Unconscious and the proletariat are emigrating to subtropical latitudes. The great ideologies, like the big companies, are relocating to the Third World.

J. K., a psychoanalyst, speaks of 'a collective Unconscious in collusion with the terrorists'. Yet she should know something about this: namely, that it is ridiculous to condemn the 'collusion' of the Unconscious with any political act whatever, and hence to submit it to a moral judgement.

Does J. K. dream of a politically correct Unconscious?

September 11th revealed not only the fragility of global power, but also an intellectual caste at odds with itself, and desperately seeking to rescue its right of oversight. But it is increasingly difficult to rescue the order of discourse in this disorder of things. All the more so as terrorism has no more meaning or clear consequences than it has objective causes. As much as a violence in the realm of things, it is a disorder of reason. The acting-out to which it attests is something quite other than the current events that result from it (including war).

Humanity needs injustice, which it can savour through the bitterness, the self-directed *Schadenfreude* that is one of the variants on the spectrum of misfortune. This mortification is particularly noticeable among the most celebrated, who like to see themselves as betrayed and misunderstood.

It is the practice of evil, and hence, in a sense, the inhuman[8] that is the distinctive mark of the human in the animal kingdom.

The definition of man is narrowing to the point of merging with his mastication coefficient, his loadbearing polygon, his basic metabolism and his intelligence quotient.

Traditionally, it has been consciousness that has made the suffering and
death of the human being more moving than that of other living creatures.
But that consciousness is a privilege and suffering is its mirror. Animals and
inanimate living things are not even granted one, which makes their annihi-
lation the more unjust (the thousands of trees felled in the forest, lined up
like corpses in a mass grave), their sacrifice the more poignant.

The destinies are equalling up today, for the suffering of human beings
has become similar to that of beasts and trees: it too has nothing to exchange
itself for; nothing redeems it any more in some other (even inner) world. The
inhuman condition of the 'inferior' creatures has become our own. And this
makes us more sensitive to the suffering they endure.

Thirty thousand years ago there lived 'another human species' – the
Neanderthals. Tremendous.

If it is true, it is symbolically more important than the fact that man is
descended from the apes. The shadow of this vanished human species weighs
heavy on all our anthropology, since our entire concept of evolution privileges the exclusive universality of a single humanity: ours, the one that survived. And what if it were not the only one? Then that's the end of our
privilege. If we had to eliminate this twin, this prehistoric double, to ensure
our hegemony, if this other species had to disappear, then the rules of the
game of being human are no longer the same.

And where does this passion for universality come from, this lust to
eliminate every other race? (It is a good bet that if any other race emerged
from space, our first aim would be to subjugate or destroy it.) Why is it that
in twin forms there always has to be one that dies? Why do we always have
to wipe out duality everywhere to establish the monopoly of a species, a race,
a subject?

Having said this, it is not certain that we really did win out. What if we were carrying that double within us like a dead twin? And perhaps many others, in a kind of Unconscious, the stubborn heir to all the previous murders. Having achieved the unity of the species, for the greater glory of *Homo sapiens*, are we not now duplicating ourselves for the worse – in that artificial twinness of the clone, in which the species, denying its origins once and for all, prolongs itself as spectre in an infinite repetition? Over the screen of our consciousness and our Unconscious hovers the shadow of this original crime, the traces of which we shall doubtless never recover.

A general tendency to invisibility as veil, to conformism as blindness. To see nothing so as not to be seen. Even architecture behind its glass façades is becoming blind and sightless. Everything shares in this phantasm of being eclipsed, of escaping the mirror stage, thanks to the screen of transparency.

In the exhibition at the Louvre on 'Painting and Crime', photos of Auschwitz are shown alongisde bloody videos by the Vienna Actionists. Isn't this a worse profaning of the Shoah than holocaust-denial?

Any value system transferred en bloc into the ritual space of discourse, like any object transferred into the ritual space of the museum, becomes a 'ready-made'.

The eternal question from the other: What am I to you? What are you to me? A veiled challenge, to which the only response is clearly: You are everything to me! I am everything to you!
Each would like to be everything to the other – each would like to be

everything to himself/herself (since, ultimately, the crucial question is: what am I to myself?).

The sad thing is that it's impossible as soon as you ask the question: there is a gulf separating the question from the response, as deep as the gulf that separates us from the other. The best thing, then, would be never to try to clarify the matter – as it was best for Orpheus never to turn around to Eurydice after emerging from the Underworld.

All around us – objects, places, towns, landscapes, faces – ask us this same metaphysical question: what am I to you?

Not only living creatures, but inanimate ones – everything makes this total demand. A kind of jealous reciprocity, to which we respond, most often, with a profound indifference. But objects too know – and know better than we do – to move off and remain silent.

Actual reality is no longer even actual enough to preserve the differential of the dream. This already tends to vanish on waking. Now, daytime consciousness exists only by this nocturnal transfusion of dreams. Their extinction is a prelude to the extinction of night in a future universe.

In fact, history is over for us, in the sense that it is unfolding on its own, on automatic pilot, and most often in a loop: we are through the looking glass of history, in a disembodied present. But the others, those who haven't experienced this stage, can only aspire to history or, possibly, destroy its symbols – including Western power, in which everything that has assumed the form of history culminates.

Those who have not entered it want history. And, to console them, we palm it off on them on a spare-part basis, like a second-hand vehicle or an assembly line.

The most idealistic, the most pre-Raphaelite form of terrorism is certainly that of the Secret Agent (Conrad), that anarchist who wanted to blow up the Greenwich meridian – to free the people from Time.

You can caress a dream, like a domestic cat. You cannot caress reality; it is like a wildcat.

The Red Cedar of Vancouver. It is six hundred years old and can expect to live until the twenty-seventh century. There is something disturbing about finding yourself in front of a living thing which you know will be there in six centuries' time. As though it had already survived you. You feel dead in advance, and yet so far removed (a spatial depth, measurable in light-years) that all anxiety is dispelled. You even feel a little immortal through this tree that has survived so many of its descendants. There is no equivalent in the human species; no one lives to be proportionately as old as the four-thousand-year-old spruces of deepest Arizona.

Just as the dying are cryogenized in the expectation that they will be resuscitated when we have acquired the key to curing their illness, we should preserve major criminals in liquid nitrogen and revive them when we have discovered the secret of justice.

In a conference on humanism: the Westerners contest universal values, against a background of colonization and historical guilt. Only the black participants speak up for the values in whose name they were enslaved.
Colonial reason is whitewashed by the blacks.

When some dream only of transforming the world, others, regarding it as having disappeared, dream only of obliterating its traces.

The real considered as infantile disorder of the virtual.
Thought considered as infantile disorder of artificial intelligence.
The image considered as infantile disorder of representation.

Seeing Nanterre and the university again twenty years on. It's like revisiting the haunts of one's childhood. Everything seems smaller. *Les événements* too have shrunk away to nothing. The inspiration that had expanded these walls, the words that had transfigured this place have vanished. But the memory of the event is intact.

Die äussersten Dinge mit der äussersten Gelassenheit sagen: to say extreme things with extreme composure.

There is as little reason to speak of corruption in the political order as of perversion in the psychical order. Our entire mental universe may be said to be perverse: there are in it only defences and evasions, phantasms and duplicity, not to mention obsession and cruelty, *ressentiment* and the many different nuances of character. Everything about it is immoral. That is how it is, end of story. Any attempt at mental regulation is as pointless as the endeavour of moralizing the social world. The balance is always, as Mandeville rightly said, that of evil by evil.

Ideas do not give forth light and their light source is elsewhere.
But they have a shadow and that shadow moves with the sun.

Our idea is that pleasure – and freedom – are positive values and that they are to be preferred, even if they are inflicted on you. That is doubtless true in terms of a vulgar economy of happiness, but it is not at all true at the symbolic level. When Afghan women are forced to remove their veils 'spontaneously', that is a violation.

Giving pleasure forcibly is worse than taking it forcibly. Forcing someone to be free is worse than enslaving them. Naturally, this is not grasped in the simplistic vision of human rights.

Satan and witches. If they admit they are in league with him, then they are disobeying him (since he forbids them to admit to being witches) and they are spared. Those who protest their innocence are burned.

A bus driver who falsely claims to have been assaulted is found guilty of wasting police time. A police spokesman declares: 'We already have so many problems with genuine violent crime. What are things coming to if we have to deal with the fake kind?' It is for this reason that a fake hold-up was in the past punished more severely than a real one, for faking evil is even more serious than evil. The hoax is evil raised to the second power.

And faking good? Isn't a fake 'good deed' worse than a bad one?

'Being out of luck'. In French, we say *'jouer de malheur'*: the accumulation of setbacks ends up becoming a game and imparting a different twist to ill fortune. You cannot say the same of good fortune: there is never an ironic twist to the excess of good fortune. One always thinks one deserves it.

Nothing stranger and more pathos-laden than the Sunday morning *Marché de la Création* on this Paris boulevard. A fine selection of kitsch and daubs, without exception, from the most abstract to the most academic. But the mystery remains because it is just as difficult to say in what way these are daubs and so many other paintings, in the private and public galleries, are 'masterpieces'. The Sunday artists exchange remarks about art that are just as senseless, though less pretentious, as those heard at the top private viewings. Where are the differentiating criteria? There is none that is objective. They are all criteria of legitimacy. One has to know how to infiltrate the subtle networks that secrete this principle of legitimacy.

The demarcation line of Art is as fierce as the demarcation line of power.

That everything exceptional is doomed to be destroyed derives from the symbolic rule that no player must be bigger than the game itself.

'The slavery of death is the root of all slavery,' says Canetti, 'and if it were not irremediable who would desire it?' An enigmatic proposition. Either: if it were possible to avoid it, no one would wish for death. Or: it is because that slavery is irremediable that so many people desire it.

Innocence, that mild form of mental deficiency, has the same aphrodisiac effect as softness of skin.

The existence of an artificial world at the very heart of reality poses no more problems than the existence of the real at the heart of an artificial universe. This is what the game show host in *The Truman Show* is saying: 'There is no more truth out there than there is in the world I created for you.' So, finally, the fact that our destiny is televisual ('We can't let him die in front of a live audience'; ' – He was born in front of a live audience') changes nothing. Everyone tends to take their environment, whatever it may be, for reality. And the more artificial it is, the more it transforms the belief in reality into a natural tendency.

A certain mix of dreams and insomnia, which may last for hours and stand in for sleep, while leaving the impression of a sleepless night.

Most often we dream in black and white and wake up in colour. Dreams are closer to early cinema (or early cinema is closer to dreams). Both are closer to the primal scene, the scene of light and shadows.

The tactile recollection of dreams: we no longer remember them, but we sense them as an object we might finger in the dark or as a vague, luminous, incomprehensible surface.

Thinking takes on first a conceptual, metaphorical form. Then a subjective, affective form. Then an animal, instinctive form. Then a reflex, automatic form. At that point, it is simply a function equivalent to the circulation of the blood and artificial respiration.

Writing is the living alternative to the worst of what it says.
There was a dramaturgy of art and language: transfiguring the real into

lyricism and violence, giving history a heroic, bloodstained ending. It seems today that art and language have the opposite function of making everything conform to ordinariness: without end and without resolution.

If the truth of what you say is in your actions, then better to give up speaking right away.

If the truth of what you think is in what you say, then better to give up thinking immediately.

If the truth of what you say is in what you don't say, then you might as well remain silent.

Saas Fee.

To live in such a place, you need an inner flame, such as Nietzsche had, a gigantic voltage differential between sublime nature and cerebral convolution. Time here is prodigiously slowed. Every second takes a minute, every minute an hour, every hour a century.

At the Happy Bar, the staff are all miserable. Even the cows howl despairingly in the fog. The village is deserted. It is raining. A single interesting figure: the whiteness of face, the hair so pale, the blue of the eyes – this Nordic type of negative beauty in which you can see the sun setting over the lakes of Finland in the faint stellar light of the wintry sky.

You can take a profound delight in horrendous things (World Trade Center) and not be happy to be so delighted. Others prefer to deny it, and take their delight without being aware of it.

'What is really happening – what I can never really see, or I will go mad – is that I am not the spider who weaves the web, and I am not even a fly caught in the web. I am the web itself, streaming off in all directions with no centre and no self that I can call my own' (James Elkins).

Cancer is the epitome of all our pathologies: the subdivision of cells to infinity provides a reflection of the proliferation of everything, and of the species itself in its transgenic frenzy.

The worm that devours the parasite that enables it to digest, and dies of it. The crustacean that wanders beneath the sea until it finds a fixed point. Once secured to that spot, it devours its own brain, which is now useless since it served it only to find this landing place.

In this same way, we devour the Nothing that enables us to digest the world, and without which we cannot survive. But we cannot prevent ourselves from doing so – just as the scorpion cannot prevent itself from killing the frog that gets it across the river.

Heavenly bodies are irresponsible – who would hold it against them? Ultimate responsibility is light years away.

Contemporary art summed up by a London taxi driver outside Tate Modern: 'When you go in, you understand why it's free.'

The powerful of this world are gathered in Rome to sign a treaty 'that puts a final end to the Cold War'. In fact they do not know they are starting a new war, of which they are the first victims: they remained parked on the tarmac, surrounded by armoured cars, barbed wire and helicopters – the whole panoply of this new cold war, the cold war of armed security, of perpetual deterrence and faceless terrorism. For the G8 at Alberta they did even better: they locked themselves away deep in a northern forest 150 kilometres from any inhabited area, in order to decide the fate of the world in all equanimity. One day they will choose to put themselves into orbit for greater security. And, later still, they will be forgotten: global power will be so distant that it will have become allegorical, as sidereal as the void that surrounds it.

Hell will be the perpetual duty of conviviality and communication: endlessly greeting people who recognize you and whom you don't recognize. The hell of the signs you no longer decipher and which you are forced to manipulate as in a dream. The hell of the ghostly ideas that signal to you from a very great distance and which you are no longer able to formulate. The hell of the words, names and faces you can't recall.

Impossible to imagine dying anywhere else than in the silence of the desert. Of all things, not to pass away amid sound and fury. To recover the only freedom, which is that of space and emptiness.

'*Die Menschen schreiben viel über das Wesen der Materie – ich wünschte, dass die Materie einmal anfänge, über das menschliche Gemüt zu schreiben.*'
'Human beings write a great deal about the essence of matter. It would be nice for matter to begin to write about the human mind' (Lichtenberg).
But isn't it already matter that writes us and thinks us – through the coming-to-pass of the world in its literalness?

Of multiple unfathomable coincidences or complicities, we say: 'It's too good to be true.' And we invoke the Unconscious. But the Unconscious itself is too good to be true. Behind all that might there not be some cruel divinity or some external fate? But we prefer the id and the drives that are the psychical reappropriation of these things. We prefer our perverse desires, our masochism and our death drive to the ill-will of the gods. If it isn't I, ego, then it's the id. If it isn't the id, it's its brother. That is always better than an external demon.

A. J. declares, in a pathos-laden flight of oratory: 'I believe in man, he is capable of anything!' Involuntary witticism: he believes he is saying man is capable of the best of things, but is he not with this same phrase saying that man is capable of the worst (though that is also just as valid a reason to believe in him)? Language retains something of the inextricable confusion of good and evil.

All imputations of nihilism and imposture originate in the same conspiracy as that of the imbeciles in the political sphere. It is in this way that imbecility flows through enlightened minds and the most open of them become the best vehicles for a stupidity that does not truly reflect who they are, but passes through them to strike elsewhere.

In the end, every molecule of the American nation will have come from somewhere else, the way a body changes cells without ceasing to be the same body. In this way America will have become black, Indian, Hispanic, Puerto Rican, without ceasing to be America. It will even be the more mythically American for no longer being so fundamentally. And all the more fundamentalist for no longer having any fundament (if indeed it ever had any, since the founding fathers themselves came from elsewhere). And all the more integrist for having become multi-racial and multicultural. And all the more imperialist for being led by the descendants of slaves.

The homily of the *curé* of Leucate on this 16 June 2002: television and the media speak constantly of evil and misfortune; they are endlessly demonizing reality. Fortunately, Pope John Paul II beatifies with abandon: 1,941 beatifications during his papacy alone – more than all the other popes put together. And, in particular, he proclaims that we are all potential apostles, like Germaine, that humble servant of Cubrac, who lived in the early seventeenth century and whose body, rediscovered intact forty years after her death, performed miracles (though a century later, the revolutionaries threw it into quicklime) and who, in the end, became Saint Germaine of Cubrac. Like that simple soul, any of us may find apostolic glory. The apostles' privileges are at an end: anyone can have his fifteen minutes of apostolic fame.

Everything here – the wind, the sun, the beach, the cliffs of Vingrau, the île Sainte-Lucie, Pla de Fitou (the white ghost of the windmills), the marvels-of-Peru, the Cathar citadels – is always sublime, but it has no echo now. It is a living memory that is brilliantly exceptional, but unreally so.

The tiredness induced by a long walk expresses itself first in a trance-like state, where insidious, aggressive thoughts bubble up without your realizing it, then in mild hallucinations, before ending in euphoric confusion.

The hypochondriacal obsession. Once all protection is secured, it is from the inside that the body is overexposed to all assaults and disruptions. Against the disorders that ensue there is only the character armour, which does not even allow the signals from the body to show through.

Wariness of one's nearest and dearest, as though they were potential witnesses for the prosecution in your existence, evidence of guilt in a trial that is permanently suspended.

The panda that is having trouble reproducing: they show him porn films to rouse his libido.

For the Japanese, the most commonplace individual and the most mundane object are both singular, even in their repetition. The problem is not to be different. For us, by contrast, that is an obligation. But there isn't difference for everyone, just as there isn't a meaning for every word (the characteristic of meaning is that not everything has it). This is how everyone ends up alone, dispossessed of both their singularity and their difference.

Intelligence is analysing things as they are.
Imagination is conceiving them as they could be.
Morality is conceiving them as they should be.
Magic is making them occur the way you conceive them.

There is no longer any interest in the mental hygiene of killers. Today we have only the mental hygiene of the victim, and the art of using one's own misfortune as a credit card.

Chirac (his puppet) interviewed on Canal Plus on *Les Guignols*,[9] then immediately afterwards on TF1 by the same presenter. In this way you can go from the false to the true simply by changing channel.

You can go from Good to Evil simply by changing scale.

You can go from the sublime to the banal by changing the lighting.

You can go from life to death without noticing.

The Meaning of Existence.

Two journalists set off to track down the Meaning of Existence throughout the world, wherever it has been sighted. Suddenly they see it loom up in the form of a very beautiful woman who boards the Orient Express and comes to sit at their table. Can you imagine that? Dining with the meaning of existence! A marvellous allegory: the meaning of existence there in flesh and blood! The ideal would clearly be to sleep with her, and they hope she is going to join them for the night. But the bitch prefers to take off with the guard. They meet up with her again at Delphi, this time in the guise of the Pythia, with the crowd of tourists who, fascinated by the Meaning of Existence and transfigured by Self-Knowledge, throw themselves off the rock into the abyss.

In the end, she simply vanishes: she was nothing but a ghost and seductress. But from time to time, here and there (for she is still at large), she signals her presence to a privileged few.

Fruttero (this fable is by Fruttero and Lucentini) recently put an end to his pursuit of the meaning of existence by throwing himself, like all the tourists dazzled by self-knowledge, down the lift shaft.

Paris-Plage: the operation would be perfect if an oil slick drifted in to pollute this pretty little beach. Then the illusion would be total: the beach attendants would be transformed into ecological clean-up agents; they would have stopped sunbathing stupid.

WTC: no trace of the bodies of the 3,000 victims. It's as though they had been dropped into quicklime. All the images without the sound, silent, vitrified, pellicularized. The scrap metal and the rubble are auctioned off. The event has more or less vanished into thin air.

The pope has reached the state of 'martyr', that is to say, of witness: witness to the possibility that the human race can live beyond death. Living experience of brain-death, of spirituality on a life-support system, of automatic piloting of the vital functions in their death throes.
A great model for future generations.

Gregory of Nyssa: 'The audacious demand of the soul is to take its pleasure face-to-face. The voice of God grants what is requested by what it refuses. God would not have shown Himself if the sight of Him were such as to arrest the desire of the seer. Therein consists the true vision of God'.
The audacious demand of man is to take his pleasure body-to-body. Woman grants what is requested only by what she refuses. She would not give herself if man's enjoyment were to be such that she would have arrested his desire. Therein consists the 'true vision of woman.'

When he has cured the patient, it is the shaman who must give something in exchange. Having made good the body, he must make good the debt.
Or the Japanese story of the woman who lets the girl drown because,

she says, if she saves her life, the child will owe her such an obligation it will be unbearable.

Our entire psychology fails before these ancestral rules.

Already God existed only in the desperate attempt to prove his existence. It is the same today with human beings, whose existence we attempt desperately to verify by the very means that make it improbable.

Feminism, populism, humanism: all words with the suffix '-ism' are the caricature of their root. Of women, of the people, of the human. Including terrorism: the caricature of terror?

In the past, the British ensured their hold on the whole of East Africa by way of their 'crusade' to abolish slavery, breaking up traditional society by emancipating the slaves (*Memoirs of an Arabian Princess from Zanzibar*).[10] Everywhere today we see the same crusade against wrongdoers, infidels, renegades against the gospel of modernity. Emancipation from the veil, sexual emancipation and the emancipation of trade are the drip-feed of global domination.

The global power's domination of the rest of the world mirrors the hegemony of the human race over other living creatures. Now, it is not clear how this 'superiority' of the human species over all the others would be given up.

Indifference to politics is said to be due to the disintegration of the social bond. In fact, it is quite the opposite. It is the wide scope for action within civil society and the intensification of communication networks – together with the promotion of a freedom whose perpetual benefits we enjoy, but of which we no longer have the concept – that create the absenteeism from oneself and from others of which political absenteeism is merely a symptom.

Lévi-Strauss used to talk about the '*signifiant flottant*', the 'floating signifier' of language. We might speak today of the '*insignifiant flottant*', the floating in-signifier of politics: mass political indifference – not even protest, but refractoriness. And what it refracts is the hidden side of politics, the side that eludes the artificial light of the electoral system.

He suddenly felt a pain that was as violent as if it were real.

Existence, similar to the stucco angel whose extremities meet in a curved mirror, comes back, almost by necessity, to a state of radicality and silence. The ideal existence is the one that lasts long enough to come back to this point of origin.

Those who forge straight ahead will never know where they have come from.

Strange disappearance of the idea of solitude, of the pathos of solitude. No one speaks of it any more, no one feels it any more. There is today only psychical isolation, mental, sensory insulation. Everyone is deterritorialized, or rather extra-territorialized from inside. The melancholy tone has disappeared.

Isolation and insularity are states of fact. Solitude was a state of mind.

The gripping narrative, minute by minute, of the people trapped in the upper storeys of the World Trade Center – thanks to the mobile phone, which became the means of communication with the dead. As gripping as the televisual collapse of the Twin Towers. If the images fulfilled the desire to enjoy the spectacle of the catastrophe live, from the outside, these real-life echoes of certain death correspond to a different phantasm: that of having lived that indescribable death from the inside – the illusion of experiencing the event to the end, from the inside, intensifying the sense of good fortune at having escaped it.

But this transfiguration is never perfect: one would have had to have died there oneself. Unlike Auschwitz, of which it has been said that the only true witnesses were those who did not return and hence have never spoken of it, in this case those who were stuck up there had the time to speak from the interior of death.

We ask computers to become intelligent or, in other words, conscious of their operation. Yet what is the consciousness of a machine but the pale allegory of the will of its programmers? (The same has been said of God and his creature: what is the consciousness of man but the pale reflection of the will of his creator?)

But haven't human beings had enough of their own consciousness anyway? Why deck machines out with it? Except to be rid of it? Passing consciousness and intelligence on to machines so as to be rid both of machines and intelligence.

'Shalmaneser', the supercomputer of *Stand on Zanzibar* doesn't need a consciousness as added extra.[11] It has its own form of jubilation and operates without thinking. To rig it out with a consciousness is to push it to suicide: it can no longer even see itself as a machine.

A mad idea is to manipulate apes genetically to the point where they conceive the idea of suicide, which was previously the prerogative of human beings. The ape is developed to the point where it prefers to kill itself because it can no longer even see itself as an ape.

This is what human beings are currently testing out on themselves by carrying themselves beyond their specific sphere, where they, like the ape, will be left with only the solution of suicide, and for the same reason: because they will no longer be able to see themselves as human beings.

Remove a single variable, to see the effect this change has on the interaction between all the variables. Remove a value, a single one, from the value system. Remove the words from language one by one: a mental technique, that of the Messianic International. Remove a tower block or two from the global landscape. To see.

The generations steeped in the virtual will never have known the Real. But that is not so serious if we accept that the Real is merely a referential illusion. More serious is the case of those who, steeped in sex and images of sex, will never have known pleasure. But this is nothing in relation to the possibility, for future generations, of never knowing death.

With so many spectacles, festivals, symposiums, art fairs and book fairs, the desire for a sudden cultural recession, or at least for a period of latency, for long enough to recover the savour of a book or the silence of images.

Zero (degree zero, zero risk, Ground Zero, zero deaths) is the current form of perfection, empty, sterile and faultless. It is the nil-sum equation, defined by the elimination of all variables. In this sense, there is no longer any difference between the perfection of life and that of death.

That nothing as extraordinary as September 11th can happen for a very long time gives us a certain sense of immortality. It will stand in as a future for us – for a time.

'*Was daraus kommt, wie von Gottes Wink, das wissen wir nicht*' (Hölderlin).

'What will come of it, as if by a sign from God, we know not.'

You can't ask someone who has himself become an icon for a solution to the problem of the image.

Does the power of anti-matter come from its being able to annihilate matter while obeying the same laws, or does it not in fact obey the same laws at all?

Does any opposing power enter into the same game as the order it destabilizes or does it destabilize it by changing the rules of the game?

Relatively speaking, September 11th will have had the same impact as the asteroid 65 million years ago, following which a kind of nuclear winter spread over the planet, causing innumerable species to disappear, but also new ones to emerge. Unfortunately, the latter were most often smaller in scale and it can hardly be otherwise with the human race and social groups. What lies in wait for us, then, in this sort of anthropological winter, is the rarefaction of forms, favouring a proliferation of elementary organisms.

The little orange, trapezoidal, translucent sail on the river, the boatmen keeping their balance. Further on, the bride in her palanquin, and the husband on horseback ahead of her. A whole parade of luminous figures. In fact, what we have here is a fake traditional Korean wedding and a TV shoot. But whether or not the ritual is authentic, there is the same racial beauty in all the faces.

The Diagonal of the Madman,
The Parallax of Evil,
The Ecliptic of Sex,
The Hypotenuse of Death.

Given the low likelihood of a meeting in this life or a future existence, the only hope is for a meeting in a previous life.

The illusion of travel is that things seem more singular as they move away from their centre of gravity. But that illusion is precious.

Overflying the deserts of Siberia. Through the mist acting like frosted glass, the sun picks out the circumvolutions of countless rivers as though with a fine paintbrush. The snakelike lines of the tiniest streams, stretching over hundreds of miles. The smallest liquid surface is a transparency viewer.

The temptation to fulfil all desires was, in the past, that of evil; temptation by the devil. Today it is good which presides over that fulfilment, but it is no longer the fulfilment of a desire or an impulse of our own. We no longer aspire to anything; we are aspirated, sucked up, by the void.

The logic of distinction is, ultimately, a precious vestige of the bygone time of signs and sign-value, the loss of which, though imperceptible in the equivalence of images, is even more serious than the loss of the real.

Prestige, challenge, rivalry, privileges – it was, at bottom, the golden age of symbolic violence, the only antidote to democratic erosion and the great game of equality of opportunity. It is doubtless as absurd to wish to eliminate that violence as any other.

Is it better to stop the haemorrhage and live in a state of perpetual transfusion?

Dreaming that he is awarded a literary prize and sells a hundred thousand copies of his book, Italo Svevo adds that naturally something which can be imagined with such exactness does not actually need to happen.

A crazy scene.
Glass-fronted terrace at pavement level, Montparnasse.
A homeless man turns up, balancing on his crutches, with one foot in plaster. Suddenly he throws one of his crutches down on the pavement. In full view, as though he had dropped it. And he waits. Not for long. Immediately a charitable person rushes to pick it up and give it back to him. It is then that he rejects it, sniggering, deriding the benefactor with an obscene gesture. Difficult to convey the violence of the scene, which lasts for half an hour. If they put the crutch next to him on the table, he knocks it off with the back of his hand and waits for the next fall-guy to come along.

The passers-by have varied reactions to the insult. They are stupefied – some mortified, others almost embarrassed by this act of conventional charity, all shocked by the merry cynicism with which he re-sets his trap, awaiting his next victim.

When he has had enough, he picks up his crutch and wanders off unconcerned. Where will he end the night? Was it a performance (a candid camera stunt)? But no: he really looked like a refugee from the *Threepenny Opera* and there was no air of modish provocation about him. His mockery was much too straightforward and fierce. Participation assured, total contempt.

A Buñuel-style act, an act of barbarous, calculated innocence. Calling to mind that story of Dostoevsky telling Turgenev that he once raped a little girl. 'Why are you telling me this?' asks Turgenev. 'Because I despise you . . .'

Once the analysis of causes is complete, everything is as it was: the pain, the disillusionment, the desire . . . In fact, causes are merely a diversion, effects have not the slightest interest in them.

A recent documentary supposing that the first pictures taken on the moon in 1969 were in reality filmed – by Stanley Kubrick – some time before in a studio near London.[12] Opprobrium rains down on the media: this is morally unacceptable! You have no right to toy with reality in this way, especially now that it has become part of world heritage. An offence against reality is worse than offending against public decency.

Yet that version, even if objectively false, is much closer to a truth than if it were authentic. It keeps us alert to the truthfulness of all the 'facts' we are presented with.

It is entirely as though God had abandoned all responsibility for the world he created, and which he is resolved now merely to watch as a disgusted spectator.

He is, ultimately, no longer anything but the expression of our resignation at this unacceptable world.

Borges: 'Nazism suffers from unreality, like Erigena's hells. It is uninhabitable; men can only die for it, lie for it, kill and wound for it. No one, in the intimate depths of his being, can wish it to triumph. I shall hazard this conjecture: Hitler wants to be defeated. Hitler is collaborating blindly with the inevitable armies that will annihilate him . . .'[13]

This applies word for word to global, comfortable, imperial civilization. In the central solitude of those very people who profit by it, it is unliveable. And all are secretly won over to the forces that will destroy it.

At the Commission of Special Dispensations and Silence.
At the Bureau of Protests and Desires.

Isabelle arrives on the TV set with a deep plunging neckline to condemn the prostitution of the female body in advertising and pornography. And why not? There is no contradiction in a *chienne de garde*[14] making herself seductive and sensual.

The hypocrisy is in the confusion of the iconic woman with the real one. Isabelle, the *chienne*, with her transparent *crêpe de velours* and her plunging neckline, is very real, though she advances behind a veil.[15] It is only in unveiling her ideology that she prostitutes herself.

Astrophysicists, microphysicists, stop harassing matter and making it confess to anything in the name of gratuitous hypotheses. Close your eyes to the cosmos, in the same way as the anthropologists, seized with remorse, have already done to the indigenous tribes lost for centuries in the depths of the jungle.

For people of a certain age in this country, culture comes free of charge. It is thought they are too old to misuse it.

The prostitution of the male body in fashion puts an end to the last heroic privilege of woman – that of being sacrificed to the gaze while concealing herself, precisely thereby, in a second nudity.

A fantastic advance by women on the path to total parity: no limits to sexual equality any longer. You can see this too in the picture of the young American woman turned torturer in the jails of Iraq, holding the naked or hooded Arab on a leash, as in some Western, women-only club.

Advancement is irresistible. It happens for better and for worse.

Parallax. *In astronomy*: the difference between the real position of a star and its apparent position, and the angle between the two. And hence also the incidence of the change of position of the observer on the observation of an object.

In photography: viewfinder parallax, the photographed image being offset from the object in the viewfinder. The discrepancy is not purely a technical one. It is, for the object, a product of the very fact of being photographed.

An object so uneven and unbalanced from inside that it cannot even stand up against a wall. It has no vertical to the ground or centre of gravity. So it thwarts all forms of stability.

I am speaking, of course, of a theoretical object.

Death is only ever that free future we dream of when we put off everything and consign all things to their future occurrence.

Objectively, the world is an illusion: it can only appear to us. Subjectively, it is the opposite: we regard it spontaneously as real.

But one may propose the opposite: subjectively, the world is an illusion of our senses. Objectively, it has force of reality.

Asymptote, clinamen, parallax, metalepsis – these are dance patterns, this is a whole non-linear geometry of theoretical space.

Patterns of near-contact and reversal, of approaching the truth without ever succumbing to it.

The cultural greenhouse effect: the toxic cloud caused by emissions from millions of museums, galleries, festivals, conferences and symposiums is much more catastrophic than the disappearance of the ozone layer. The asphyxia caused by the activity of thousands of creative brains damages the quality of life more certainly than all the world's industrial pollution.

And if no Tokyo Congress has yet managed to control technological pollution, what body could put a brake on cultural nuisance?

Language is expatriating itself into words that are afraid to mean anything.

We can bear ideas and events only when laundered by commentary, like the dirty money concealed by banking secrecy.

'In the heart and the belly it continues to sing its poisonous song – Better to kill a child than to harbour unsatisfied desires within oneself' (Kenzaburo Oe).

Ressentiment is an empty, useless passion only if it assumes a sentimental form.

What establishes the rule, and confirms it, is the exception. So we may conceive of a rule made up only of exceptions (that, says Lichtenberg, is the ideal rule).
But that is true only of moral and grammatical rules. There is no exception to the symbolic rule.

The tragedy of insomniacs is that they no longer even have the possibility of dreaming of reality – like S. J. Lec – or, therefore, of knowing the relief of escaping from it by waking.

Someone who had slipped entirely from my memory turns up fifty years later. It is like a line drawn between two lives, a shuttle movement of time's arrow. Everything in-between seems to have happened in the twinkling of an eye.

According to a statistical study, fifty per cent of statistics are wrong. So, if this statistic is itself fifty per cent wrong, does this mean that only twenty-five per cent of statistics are wrong or that twenty-five per cent are correct? This is how it is with calculations embedded within others and, more generally, with calculations of probability, from which all logical distinction has disappeared.

There is something worse than being unmasked: not being unmasked.
Thus the crime will have kept on leaving clues, and illusion itself cannot bear to remain illusion. It is constantly prostituting itself to the world and actualizing itself in full view.

Thinking is as difficult as walking in the snow without leaving tracks. Or else you have to go back over your tracks step by step, like the child in *The Shining*, pursued by his father in the labyrinth of ice.

Political power exists only because we want absolutely none of it. And the political sphere is there only to mask this defection on our part by a *trompe-l'oeil* system of representation.
But life, such as it is, we want too. And force, potency. That too we want, irresistibly. But perhaps less deeply than we want its opposite.

Unconditional praise of life and happiness. *Existenz über alles!*
This fierce optimism, this idealism, which sees the worst catastrophes, the worst corruption as having a right to claim mitigating circumstances.

The critical spirit is not dead, contrary to the opinion of the Enlightenment nostalgics. It has simply metabolized into all the ironic procedures, all the sardonic artifices in which we play, smugly, on our own incredulity. 'The Last Man, talking to himself while shaking his head incredulously,' said Nietzsche.

Excess today, our contemporary *'hubris'*, is the excess of universal hybridization – like the fluorescent rabbit that is a cross between a rabbit and an octopus – and of making everything copulate with itself like the *crepidula fornicata*.[16]

All this televisual conditioning: make-up, spotlights, image-feed, monitors . . . anguish. Never any silence, any slip-ups or sighs. You switch on your tele-prompter and set yourself to automatic pilot. The studio lights and the night in your head.
Exactly the opposite of the night hours when ideas are close to waking dreams.

War means destroying the enemy's quality of light.

Who would come and sit next to you in a near-empty cinema, except someone with criminal intent?

Transsexuality: what was a psychotic hallucination has become one of our human rights. Might it not rather be human rights that have become a psychotic hallucination?

Silicon breasts, which never subside, even when horizontal.
Silicon thought, the sort that never gets flabby and that stands up on its own in any context.

The lesson to be drawn from X's fatal fall after leaving a moronic show: only go to shows where you would not mind dying immediately after seeing them.

One cannot reasonably trust in the will, that 'rational' strategy that works only one time in ten. One has, rather, to clear the decks around a decision, leave it hanging, then let oneself slide into it, as though being sucked in, with no thought for causes and effects. To be willed by the decision itself; in a sense, to give in to it. The decision then becomes a self-fulfilling prophecy.

They estimate that it cost 25 million dollars to prepare the World Trade Center attack. The budget for a future film of the same event is put at 250 million dollars.
Fiction is far more expensive than reality.

Choose: of all wars, the one that will not take place.
Of all possibilities, the least probable.

Of all concepts, the most inconceivable.
Of all meditations, the most untimely.
Of all possible enemies, the one beneath all suspicion.

The noise of the paint cracking, at night, along the walls.
The silence of the dust, rippling and slithering from one wall to the next.
The cry of the mirror when the impact of the image strikes.

The language of the weather forecast is as rigged as that of politics. Distilled panic, blackmailing with safety . . . 'The elements are raging' (no, it is the safety measures that are raging). 'The snow is late'!

Prevention, contraception, forceps, abortion, miscarriage, phantom pregnancy, cloning and twinning – the paradigm of obstetrics and gynaecology is present everywhere in current events.

Blanchot is dead and the homages are raining in.[17]
He will have lost his gamble of effacing effacement, and his proselytes and commentators will, in the very glorification of silence, have missed a fine opportunity to be silent. He could not have been unaware, himself, that his self-effacement made him an object of insatiable curiosity (of an ironic kind, of course!), a thwarted great game, the absolute snobbery of absence.
Ultimately, though, Blanchot (like Duchamp) is the original and all the rest is a joke. All this subtle, non-academic philosophy, imbued with his ideas, all this philosophically correct philosophy of the unsaid, the forbidden

and the inexpressible in the end merely reaps the dividends of an experience of thought that is not its own.

Moreover, there is no need whatever to be a philosopher to play that particular game (self-effacement). Everyone effaces himself but no one speaks about it. The entire history of ordinary life is one of an effacement much more radical than that of thought yearning to disappear.

Simple folk, the uneducated, the artless *are* the thought of Blanchot. *They* have succeeded in effacing effacement. The philosophical exigency is embodied in those who know nothing of it.

Being secondarily pessimistic – believing that the good always ends up going bad. And secondarily optimistic – believing that the system is best placed to put an end to itself.

After the three great revolutions – Galileo and the end of geocentrism, Darwin and the theory of evolution, Freud and the 'discovery' of the Unconscious – our contemporary revolution is that of the virtual and of information technology, and it distances man increasingly from sovereignty over the natural world, of which he was the centre in the days when the earth did not yet revolve around the sun, in the days when he was not yet descended from the apes. He is becoming increasingly eccentric today – a peripheral, artificial extension of his own model.

The modern form of negative theology: reality can be defined only by what it is not, and what it is not is precisely *the world as it is*, which is not in any sense the real world.

There are many ways of being witty and intelligent – almost as many as of not being. They are often the same.

Like free electrons on the planet of the apes, with a time window on to a parallel universe.

The only solution to the mechanization of man is *le devenir-machine*: becoming-machine. Warhol had seen this. He was the apotheosis of the machinic: total automatism, all trace of the human gone.

The dream of the virtual era, by contrast, is to wrest the machine from machinicity, to make it intelligent and soulful, 'interactive', to turn it into an associate 'anthropoid' with the same affective and intellectual, sexual and reproductive functions – and, lastly, the same viruses and melancholia.

Beyond a certain speed, a body no longer seems to be propelled, but rather sucked along by the void. A fine metaphor for desire and seduction: desire is a drive, seduction is a strange attraction.

The trout ascending the waterfall does not do so by sheer effort. It does not battle against the flow. The water hurtling down in free fall creates, at the heart of the swirling waters, a suction pulling in the opposite direction. The trout seeks out this ascending flow and lets itself be carried upwards.

Intertwined spiral of life and death – much more difficult to decipher than the spiral of DNA.

'In short, gentlemen, we are all hermaphrodites, divided animals, as much in our being as in our knowledge and our principles' (Siegfried Lenz).

In the cinema studios in Vancouver, it is specified contractually that no one must look the stars in the eyes, 'for fear of disturbing them or breaking their concentration'.

The most perfect synthesis of theory and practice is the vanishing of thought into the actual course of the world.

'These thoughtless men who love life and do not see that their mistress cheats on them every day with death' (Schnitzler).

All these dreams of helplessness, distress, of forking paths, of being locked up miles from anywhere, all these confused, indescribable episodes, are expressions of the fact that one is coming close to a secret zone, an impassable line – not at all, as the conventional interpretation has it, the bar of repression, but something more subtle of which *we* are the repressed.

Right across the species, everything must be stored away and put under seal – including the famous genome – doubtless for the use of a later race, who will exploit it as fossil material. We shall ourselves, by the combined pressure of the mass of computer data and the continental drift, be transformed into a metamorphic deposit (the Unconscious already seems like a psychical residue of the Carboniferous). Right now, one has the impression the human race is merely turning in on itself and its origins, desperately gathering together its distress flares and dematerializing to transform itself into a message.

But a message to whom?

Everyone is looking for a safe area, some form of permanent plot that can eclipse existence as a primary abode and protect us from death.

The unfortunate thing is there aren't even any plots held in perpetuity in the cemeteries any more.

Double blindness: deluding oneself with the hope that Le Pen will disappear – in the illusory belief of recovering an elusive democracy – and not seeing that Le Pen is, in himself, of no importance.

Yet the problem he poses is all the more important for that. For, if it is true that he represents nothing (he is not alone in that!), he thereby personifies all those who no longer even have the idea of being represented, who can no longer even imagine any kind of political order whatever.

Now, there can no longer be any question of 'refounding politics' on those ruins, those vestiges of representation. We must go to the very end of politics, even in its most regrettable consequences for 'the social order'. The political class, both Left and Right, is incapable of doing this – incapable of managing the accursed share that is at the heart of the social.

The truth is that the only current political message comes from beyond the political sphere, whoever the messenger.

To be operational, you have to have put all useless complexity out of action. You have to have determinedly simplified your mental functioning. It is in this way that you respond best to an environment that is itself simplified and operational, where the mirror has been turned into a phase, pleasure into a principle and death into a drive.

After centuries of veiled seduction and concealment of the body, the overexposure of sex and nudity merely gives the illusion there was a secret there and it has been unmasked.

It is like truth, which one deludes oneself one discovers, whereas it is thought itself that produces truth as its justificatory horizon.

He who has everything will keep what he has. From him who has nothing, even that will be taken away.

Philosophy leads to death, sociology leads to suicide.

Shrivelled anus, short-windedness, limp member, short-sightedness, angioplastied ventricle, urethral polyps – but a clear, hard head.

Best joke of the Iraq war: it wasn't Saddam's statue they knocked down, but his double's! It wasn't the war that was won either, but the ghost of a war. Saddam disappears behind his many doubles – the war disappears behind the signs of war.

The car transforms everyone into a potential delinquent, but at the same time into a potential cop. The car awakens in each of us the slumbering killer and the sleeping policeman.

The worst thing is when each citizen begins to be his own policeman. If there are vigilantes, surely it's to rid us of vigilance?

2001: A Species Odyssey

The absurdity of all these paleontological productions in which everything is directed towards man as the goal. A chimpanzee always looks as though it's an extra in an animal costume (it is, in fact, here a man dressed up as an anthropoid). As Napoleon showed through beneath Bonaparte, so *Homo sapiens* showed through beneath the coelacanth. And our successive ancestors have, ultimately, no other quality than having played their part in our definitive advent. Whilst, with Darwinian theory, man found himself annexed to animality, in this restitution, by contrast, the entire animal chain finds itself annexed to the human by a kind of reverse evolutionism. Reconquest of the origins of man in the light of his ultimate domination.

The illusion still holds for the most distant forms, for animals are increasingly fascinating as one plunges into the immemorial past: like the dinosaurs, they tip over into pure mythology. Things go wrong when, over time, the saga becomes a 'realist' animation, a soap opera in which the racism of the victors shines out retrospectively. As, for example, in the marvellous encounter in which the hairy Neanderthal primate is overwhelmed by the Cro-Magnon showgirls who, make-up and all, already have the Hollywoodian features of the higher race.

'But you're not free to prefer an inferior cultural stage. Every culture has to keep pace with the general trend,' says the Empire's emissary to the dissidents of Williamson's world (Philip K. Dick).[18] And he is indeed right to destroy this civilization, which has chosen to develop as a craft-based society rather than conform to the technical norms of the global order. For the slightest exception, even inoffensive, is a heresy and a mortal threat to the whole. Once the system has applied that law to itself, it cannot but impose it on the others.

One exception: the tribe in the Philippines that the anthropologists decided not to study so as not to alter its structure. A relinquishment of the right to draw up the universal inventory, but one that in no way challenges the privilege of the dominant culture: the natives will live in a state of artificial survival from now on within the museum-like frame of universal culture. They will serve as living fossils.

Cloning must be sacrilege to the doctrines of metempsychosis, as it interrupts the sequence of reincarnations and the migration of souls. But it is also sacrilegious where the laws of evolution are concerned, since it is tantamount to an unlimited perpetuation of the species.

In the body, a will to help begins to form. It is the body that chooses, among the innumerable pathogenic elements at its disposal, the illness that will purify you by diet and fever.

The inaugural artwork on the square in front of the Basel Art Fair: a mirror cube, in the middle of which a man is defecating. It's a two-way mirror. He can see the people around him, but they can't see him. The opposite of the peep-show: the exhibitionist hides from view and it's the spectators who are watched. The perfect image of contemporary art.

You want to turn the situation around, as is always the case with looking. You want to look intensely from outside, and hence without seeing, at the centre of the cube, where the defecator is sitting. He would see you watching him and, while knowing you can't see him, I'm sure he could not bear that gaze.

The same potential for turning things round in a peep-show. If the girl set about staring at the voyeur through the window, he is the one who would suddenly feel undressed.

In Arthur C. Clarke's short story, the stars go out one by one as soon as all the names of God are counted. Isn't this the same operation of digitization of the universe that the whole world's computers have undertaken, this time on their own account, with no regard for God? And must we not expect to see the same extinction of the world at the end of this integral calculus of reality?

Leucate. New homily on the Covenant.

First act: Moses sprinkles his people with the blood of three young bulls.

Then, at the Passover, Christ says to the Jews: 'Eat, this is my body. Drink, this is my blood'! (The Jews are taken aback by this: we are not cannibals!)

Lastly, to crown the triptych, it is Christ who sacrifices himself.

But, according to the good *curé*, we should not believe this sacrifice frees us from original sin (yet that is what the worshippers secretly believe).

Silent, rural horror of those same worshippers (who stand up, sing and cross themselves like mechanical birds) at the mention of the sacramental.

The idea that the Mass is a sacrament in which the Lord's sacrifice is renewed is like water off a duck's back to them. They come every Sunday to absolve themselves of their everyday existence, and that is the whole of their liturgy.

As for the *curé*, I've never seen him succumb to routine. He even seems at one point to take himself for Moses, when lamenting that holy water has been substituted for bulls' blood.

The Christ of Lagrasse: lascivious death throes.

When you have spent a day in Weimar, you really can say you have spent a day in Weimar. And that isn't the case in any old town. Here time really unfolds, no one second being in any hurry to get ahead of another.

Moreover, you are protected by a chorus of tutelary divinities (Goethe, Luther, Nietzsche and the others), which lend each minute an eternal dimension.

You dream of Wolfgang sending Charlotte the lover's message of a lighted candle from across the town, and Friedrich sending that of the Eternal Return.

Here, becoming is itself stilled.

The obsessive dividing up of time: the infinitesimal splitting that enables Achilles never to reach the tortoise – and hence to dodge any final term, including that of death. The more imminent it is, the more the intervening period of time is subdivided. There is still one day, one hour, one minute, one second. Each second passes, but the next one is never certain. Time tightens and condenses to the point where it no longer lets time pass. A substance so intense, so dense, that the future will not be able to pass through it. A well-counted hour will go on being counted out forever. In the film of time, this is the insane hope of a freeze-frame. And our passion for artificial image techniques no doubt derives from the fact that we can suspend the image, reverse its course or speed it up. We dream of doing the same with time (and with dreams too).

It is the same with endings as it is with death – the dream is never to arrive at them, and simultaneously to pass beyond.

'Each of the moments separating me from the ordeal seemed infinitely divisible – the particle of time to come being always the one that would enable me at last to face reality and concentrate' (Updike).

Another miracle of division: given that life expectancy is constantly increasing, we gain time against the final reckoning as we go on. Thanks to the indefinite interval involved, and applying the paradox of Achilles and the tortoise, we shall never catch up with death.
We have become virtually immortal.

Every day we lose three minutes of sunshine, but at the same time a fraction of our existences and our responsibility. Yet each day characterized by a diminution of responsibility is a red-letter day.

How things change: the South African cactus used by the Bantu in their desert to fend off hunger and thirst has nowadays become a miracle obesity cure in the USA.

The man buried with his uranium battery digital watch.
This way he will know in death precisely what time it is to one-thousandth of a second.

In that labyrinth of signage that is an airport, modern man rediscovers the anxiety of prehistoric man in the jungle.

Not understanding out of impatience to understand, out of a rushing towards meaning – like stammerers with words. Out of a rushing towards the other, whose presence clouds the issue – it is the same turmoil as when one is photographing a living creature.

Being equal to the circumstances is difficult when the circumstances are at their lowest point.
But they are never up to the mark.

The two Siamese twin sisters, joined at the cranium, but with two separate brains and hence two distinct wills. For twenty-three years they were never able to look each other in the eye. They died after the operation.

For attempting to have sexual relations with an elephant, Tram Chung Song, who had said in his defence that the elephant had suddenly seemed to him like a reincarnation of his wife, was taken at his word by the judges and sentenced to seventeen years' imprisonment – the usual sentence for marital rape.

The subject who takes himself for what he is is mad. But if he senses that he is not really what he is, then he can use that identification as a mask. This is the way it is with truth too: if you claim to possess it, you are mad. But if you know it doesn't exist, then you can make use of all the signs of truth.

'*Versuchen wir den Spiegel zu betrachten, so entdecken wir endlich nichts als die Dinge auf ihn. Wollen wir die Dinge fassen, so kommen wir zuletzt wieder auf nichts als auf den Spiegel. Das ist die allgemeine Geschichte der Erkenntnis*' (Nietzsche, *Morgenröte*).

'When we try to examine the mirror in itself we discover in the end nothing but things upon it. If we want to grasp the things we finally get hold of nothing but the mirror. – This, in the most general terms, is the history of knowledge.'[19]

'Whoever has a will of their own to invest in things will not be mastered by things; in the end, even chance events arrange themselves to meet our most personal needs. I am often surprised to see how little power even what is seemingly the most unfavourable destiny has over a will! Or, rather, I say to myself: how necessary it is for the will itself to be a destiny for it always to get the better of destiny itself' (Nietzsche).

Only metaphysical passion can compete with seduction. The one fights against the illusion of an objective reality, the other against the subjective illusion of desire.

The worst thing being to turn desire into a reality.

To consider everything from its dead angle, its blind spot: the place accidents come from.

The cyclists you pass in the forest do not respond to your gestures of friendship. The reason is that, in addition to being a cyclist, you have to look like one, you have to give off the signs of cycleity (O, Roland!): the helmet, the mask, the fluorescent cycling gear, the low-slung body position. Shame on those who give off only the signs of tiredness. But doubtless they don't even see you – being overtaken, as they ride, by *rigor mortis* and pedalling all the more stubbornly for it.

Exactly as the stars in the sky in Arthur C. Clarke's story, so the stars in one's brain go out one by one, once all the data have been stored. But perhaps this descent into the zone of silence and catalepsy is a defensive reaction against the excess of an artificial memory?

The Other should be a glorious, not a pitiful Other, an object of admiration not of commiseration, the object of a challenge, not that interactive, democratic Other which is not even really your equal.

The Other exists more intensely in the dual relation, in rivalry and challenge, than in interaction, conviviality and cosy multiculturalism.

Two lovers wish to give each other a present. But neither can afford to. She sacrifices her splendid head of brown hair to give him a platinum watch-strap. And he chooses to sell his watch to give her a box of tortoise-shell combs for her hair.

Isn't the heatwave a form of insurrection on the part of the climate itself? It can no longer bear being meteorologized, any more than the elements can bear being martyred or animals being industrialized or human life itself being programmed and normalized. Hence the revenge of bird 'flu, mad cow disease, extreme climatic effects and of human existence pushed to its limits. The aged themselves are finding a way of taking their revenge by using their deaths as a politically destabilizing factor – the only event of an unspectacular summer.[20]

Fowl pest, mad cow disease, SARS, the New York blackout, the oil slick, the heatwave – so many abnormal events, so many 'terrorist' phenomena.

It is order itself that forces us to conceive terrorism as something unlimited, since any infringement of order is condemned as such. Even natural convulsions and catastrophes are 'terrorist' in nature. What was merely a physical phenomenon has become a violation of the global order.

Against the advice of doctors, the governor refuses to allow an incurably ill man to be put out of his misery. This is the other face of capital punishment. One day we shall have to fight for the abolition of the life penalty, as we did in the past for the abolition of the death penalty.

Shadows have always preceded us, and they will outlive us. We were dead before we were alive, and we shall be again.

Glory and Performance.

Seen from America and by American intellectuals (Susan Sontag), the denial of reality in European cultures, and particularly in French theory, is merely 'metaphysical' pique at no longer being master of that reality, and the – at once arrogant and ironic – manifestation of that powerlessness. And this is no doubt true. But the converse is also true: is not the bias towards reality among Americans, their 'affirmative thinking', the naïve and ideological expression of the fact that they have, by their power, a monopoly of reality?

We do, admittedly, live with a ridiculous nostalgia for glory (the glory of history and culture), but they live with the ridiculous illusion of performance.

Intense interest in deepening the individual mystery of the other – any other, as it happens; in this sense, all are equally strange. *Our* secret is merely an open one.

At the bedside of dying reality, consciousness is merely the Extreme Unction, the last of the palliative sacraments.

If the whole world becomes Western, where will the sun rise?

The silence underfoot, on the soft earth, after yesterday's rain. The clouds scudding away with the north wind and, far above, the still sky, the long stratospheric clouds. A horizon of phantom windmills with white tentacles. The tiny black butterflies to the sides of the path have disappeared. Just the ants still there, in their prodigiously useless bustle. The wind strengthens, as though blowing from all directions at once. When it stops, here where it never stops, the stillness is preternatural.

Freed even from the obligation of having to go down to the sea. The whole day is spent at the same place. Evening falls, the hawkmoths settle on the marvels-of-Peru. The full moon rises. Hypostatic light. The hills pale in the moonlight and the silence causes space to falter.

From Copernicus to Galileo – from intuition to objectivity. Today a new division is occurring: decline of objectivity, redistribution of truth. And we come back to the starting point: the pure light of the gaze. But it is no longer the light of a human consciousness, the natural light of knowledge, but the light of the screen and numerical calculation.

Rediscovery of the beauties of the provinces – Compiègne, for example, on the occasion of Prosper Mérimée's bicentenary ('its forest, its château, its theatre'). With, as ever, the very Parisian colonial ethnocentrism. How did those people manage to live before they were discovered? As it was with the Indians: could it be that they had a soul without having heard the word of Christ?

The champions of the digital adopt an absurd line of argument (absurd in the sense of Freud's story of the kettle): 1. It is a revolution, an absolute advance. 2. At any rate, we have no choice, the process is irreversible.
But it must be one or the other: if it is inevitable, there's no point representing it as an ideal dimension. And if it's destined to win out, there's no point claiming it is best.

Any form of irony or offhandedness about one's own ideas is wounding to one's interlocutor.

If one resolves to be what one is, origins, filiation and all traces in general seem an undesirable supplement.

Naïve, captive, subliminal duplicity. Whatever happens, the double – that internalized otherness – dissociates itself from one's official being. In the face of this internal division, how is it with the unity of the real world?

The distance of the child from those who see him as innocent, the wicked delight that takes root in the form of cunning, the innate sense of having his own preserve, which will never leave him, even if he becomes a civilized being. 'The point at which the intuition forms in the child that other people exist who think differently is the point at which he learns to lie.'
Later on, he will perfect that duplicity by learning to lie to himself.

Everything is competing to show its good will. Things tend irresistibly towards perfection, effusiveness, reconciliation. Fortunately, nothing is ever perfect, thanks to Dostoevsky's 'unspeakable little demon . . . that evil spirit that prompts to murder and scorn.'
Everything tends irresistibly towards transparency. However, there remains a glimmer of secrecy – a clandestine dust-breeding that is mostly useless, an umbilical mirage, insider trading, but secret all the same.

Where America is concerned, we more or less harbour the illusion that everything that is thought over here becomes a reality over there: not just the achieved utopia of technology and happiness, but the utopia of theory become reality.

All this is based on a massive misunderstanding: theory is not made to be realized. Its effectuation is also its death. But this accomplishment allows us to glimpse what might well be an obscure desire on the part of thought: that of losing itself in its effects, of abolishing itself in a reality that transfigures or disfigures it.

This is doubtless what has happened between America and European thought: a great two-handed game, a dual relationship without absolute primacy of one party or the other – the supremacy of French thought is a mirage, even if it has lasted for a whole generation.

All in all, we might be said to have witnessed a 'becoming-phenomenon' of ideas, but in a non-Hegelian sense: not by a sublation of Spirit, but in the sense of an irrevocable derision and degradation.

And yet this ordeal has to take place: thought has to be confronted with its actualization, for better and for worse. In this sense, we can say that this confrontation of thought with its own actualized object – with which, in the guise of the real, it cannot at all reconcile itself – has constituted an event.

Narcissism isn't what it was. It was at the mirror stage, the stage of seduction. Today it is at the screen stage, the stage of 'self-processing'.

It isn't enough now to be an object of desire for oneself. You have to be an object of manipulation and performance.

The despair of women, to whom men no longer offer even the opportunity of verifying their powers of seduction. Corresponding despair of men at the women who no longer even have the desire to be seduced and who now envisage only the sexual disposal of their bodies.

While the flesh-and-blood lecturer is speaking, his double looms up behind him on a giant screen, and his words spool out like a cartoon speech bubble.

Where do the concepts and figures of analysis come from? Are they not purely and simply the metaphysical expression of a set of character traits, of an unfitness for reality and a fitness only for illusion and disillusion? Denial of reality, duplicity and intelligence of evil, ellipsis of the will and fatal strategies – might these things not all be faked? But isn't it a success to be one more spiral in the simulation?

Womankind as irreparable accident of nature (Aristotle) or as the irony in the life of the community (Hegel).[21] Following out a counter-genealogy of man and woman, one might arrive at a negative destiny of man, forever loaded down with the curse of power, and at an opposite choice on the part of women to be nothing, a fleshly absence, a form of flesh and blood disappearance – a force far superior to the political, mental power of domination.

The power of women derives from the fact that they hold the gates of the void and cede entry to men only in accordance with certain rules and at their own risk. The woman who renounces this specific quality to become a 'true being', an authentic being, an '*être-pour-jouir*', at the same time loses the benefit of this suprasensual power.

All power is obsessed by that which denies it, by that which does not miss it and whose dreams it does not haunt. The male by the female, for example. But if women were to begin to dream of a visible force, then men would cease to be obsessed with them and would in turn lose interest in femininity. If women began to dream of power, then femininity would revert to the men who knew how to lose interest in power.

Now, the whole of our current masquerade illustrates this trap set for the female by the male. Trapping women with the taste for power and authority, making them responsible, masculinizing them, in the same way as white people are forever whitening black people and decking them out in the whiteness of the universal.

In this historical to-ing and fro-ing between dominant and dominated, it is even to be feared that black people will become whiter than the white, and women more masculine than men.

Man is obsessed with woman (this does not seem to be mutual). Possession does not set him free from obsession. Above and beyond *jouissance*, his obsession with her remains. It is an obsession with something like an eternally feminine prior state, an idea or fleshly form which was there before you and will outlive you. All other obsessions refer back to this one.

It is fuelled by the secret desire to wrest from woman more than she gives you or has ever given you, to wrest from her her femininity itself. Woman-as-object is the purest expression of this obsession, since it is the object that is ungraspable. And it is in becoming-object that woman puts herself out of reach, and becomes the horizon of the obsessional desire.

Just as it would be necessary to remove many other veils to wrest from women the secret of their power, so it would take many other tortures to wrest from men the secret underlying their unafraidness of death.

As for knowledge, its source must lie in a stronger motive than that of the will, stronger even than inspiration or one's own particular genius – it must lie in some profound challenge to oneself. Knowledge is a matter of honour, like seduction. And it is astonishing that we so make it a point of honour to seduce and yet do not set anything like the same store by the demand for lucidity. For the two passions are inseparable.

Speech always begins with stammering. Acts and action always begin with trembling. There is no continuum of the will. It acts on the body by fits and starts (*stossweise*) and is the product of an interval, a rapid alternation, between tension and release: to act is to produce a difference – even a slight one – between you and yourself. If you eliminate the intervals, tetany ensues: you shake all over.

Dysphylaxia (Primo Levi): disappearance, under the effect of hyposterone, of all the immune barriers of race, species and sex. The grandmother fertilized by larch pollen whose hair falls out in autumn and grows back in spring. Exactly the phantasm of current technology: a monstrous transfusion, a universe of chimerical manipulations. The opposite of the play of metamorphosis.

Archimedes' viewpoint: 'give me but one firm spot on which to stand, and I will move the earth.' Today: 'give me one single piece of exact information, a single absolute, real fact and I will transform the world.' But in the virtual universe of information, as elsewhere in each of our random existences, that point of absolute gravity is nowhere to be found.

The less you manage to give names to the various faces, the more they come to resemble each other, the more they gesture to one another from afar in your memory.

Of the veil or unveiling, which is the most alienating, the most humiliating, the most insulting? The immense hypocrisy of all those who denounce the veil, but are quite at ease with universal pornography. In any event, the question goes far beyond the veil and the female condition. At issue is a culture of obscenity that cannot but tear away all veils – according to the imperative of transparency. At issue is the profound jealousy of a ragged culture at all the ceremonial cultures – those cultures whose signs enwrap them, whereas our culture is laid bare by its signs themselves.

This is merely the beginning of a general de-signification, in which all distinctive marks will become anathema, suspect of masking or even, quite simply, signifying something, and hence potentially terroristic. At the end of the process all that will be left will be lightweight, inoffensive signs – advertising signs or marks of the disembodied fanaticism of fashion.

That, no doubt, is where the story of the veil will end.

A mirror in which, when you look at yourself, you would see your face emerge only gradually, in ghostly fashion, as from the light-sensitive film of a Polaroid.

In nuclear reactions, in fission or fusion, it is the energy of the splitting of matter that is recovered in the form of heat. In the social and psychological spheres, it is the energy of unbinding, of the fracturing of the symbolic that is recovered in the form of 'conviviality', 'interaction' and 'human warmth'.

In the mirror of representation, as in the rear-view mirrors of cars, objects remain at a distance. If you pass through the mirror, they get dangerously close. 'Objects in this mirror may be closer than they appear.'[22]

The photographic lens captures objects beyond representation: 'what they look like as photographed', '*tels qu'en eux-mêmes la prise de vue les change*.'[23]
With digital photography, objects are no longer even wrested from representation – they are not photographed, they are pictographed.

In a Chinese film, a man is responsible for the death of a child, his friend's son. He attempts, first of all, to make amends for the death with money. The father is prepared to accept it, but the mother rejects it. She wants vengeance: the man owes her a life in exchange. He then sees no solution but to die. But the mother denies him that too easy solution, the suicide that would unbind him forever. He must, then, renounce dying. Only on these terms is the mother reconciled to him.

Those politicians who try to slip a bit of power to the 'intellectuals' (missions, commissions, etc.) – on the one hand, to prove to themselves that they have some, but, above all, so as to leave no one outside the field of power. 'If I knew that there still are on this earth some men *without any power* I would say that nothing is lost' (Canetti).

As Nerval says of hours, so it is with books: it is already the next one, it is still the last one, and it is always the only one.

I have mothballed my coat of lights, that of the desert casinos. From now on, I live in my crystal ball.

Analytic distance fades with use. Critical distance becomes the metastasis pure and simple of the reality it is analysing, which has itself become critical by capillary action and permeable to the worst of things. Positive and negative are in league like charity and cruelty, like violence and compassion.

Criticism then provides a balancing function for the system, or serves to regulate the transit, like those capsules you take to offset the side-effects. Or else, like consciousness in general, it fulfils the function of palliative care.

This comfortable, democratic, cultivated mode of life, the mode of welfare and affluence, is something we have shared for a long time innocently, without bad conscience, on the assumption that we were the search engine for the future happiness of the planet. This illusion is no longer possible today; discrimination and a global divide seem entrenched for good, and we can no longer live this lifestyle as part of a symbolic division. We now hold it only in usufruct and as annuity, and we live locked in a fortress whose only thought is to protect itself from the rest of the world.

However, the failure of this universal perspective is shared and the despair is the same on both sides of the global divide – among the richer than rich and the poorer than poor.

A poetic film: *Pleasantville.*
Passing through the TV screen and emerging into an entirely sanitized American small town, wholly in black and white, and seeing it turn to colour as passion progressively exerted its effect. Seeing fire, rain, sex and violence

resurface little by little – everything which, by its absence, characterized the translucent, achromatic hell of that ideal, virtual town.

One very fine scene is when the mother, who has secretly become involved in an adulterous love affair, illegally colours up and her son makes her up in black and white so that she can appear in public. One is reminded of the Japanese tattoo on the woman's thigh that is invisible ordinarily and shows up only with sexual excitement. One of the finest metaphors for the Unconscious.

The lack of distinction between the real and the virtual is the obsession of our age. Everything in our current affairs attests to this, not to mention the big cinematic productions: *The Truman Show, Total Recall, Existenz, Matrix*, etc.

This question has always been there behind literature and philosophy, but it has been present metaphorically, as it were, implicitly, through the filter of discourse. The 'encoding/decoding' of reality was done by discourse, that is to say, by a highly complex medium, never leaving room for a head-on truth.

The encoding/decoding of *our* reality is done by technology. Only what is produced by this technical effect acquires visible reality. And it does so at the cost of a simplification that no longer has anything to do with language or with the slightest ambivalence and which, therefore, puts an end to this subtle lack of distinction between the real and the virtual, as subtle as the lack of distinction between good and evil. Through special effects, everything acquires an operational self-evidence, a spectacular reality that is, properly speaking, the reign of simulation. What the directors of these films have not realized (any more than the simulationist artists of New York in the eighties) is that simulation is a hypothesis, a game that turns reality itself into one eventuality among others.

On Ballard: 'It is no longer to fabricate the unreal from the real, the imaginary from the givens of the real. The process will, rather, be the opposite: it will be to put decentred situations, models of simulation in place and to contrive to give them the feeling of the real . . . to reinvent the real as fiction.'[24]

Artificial intelligence is an asexual activity, in which the body is only there, as Turing says, to give the 'intelligence' something to occupy itself with.

The spiritual practice of evil – sin, destiny, punishment, death – is over. The spiritual practice of crime is over. We are now in the political economy of misfortune.

If it turns out that the coming of global power and the frantic race to totalize the world have no more meaning than the economic sphere taken overall, and all this is more a mad whirl than a rational development, isn't that another novel form of disappearance?

From an aesthetic point of view, I would propose burying wind turbines underground, as they do with high-voltage power lines.

Deep in the Brazilian forest, Alexander von Humboldt encountered a parrot that alone knew a few words of the language of a tribe entirely destroyed by smallpox.

If the world is what it is, where does the illusion of appearances come from? Whence the obsession with truth? And whence transcendence?

God is still part of the illusion of the world. But that illusion is an illusion only for consciousness, that is to say, relative to a hypothetical, indecipherable entity. It's an endless whirligig. In these conditions, it's no use trying to think you are God. That is to wish, like Münchhausen, to wrest yourself from illusion by pulling yourself up by the hair.

Thought is augural, unfinished. When it can be verified absolutely, it moves to the reflex stage, the animal stage. This is more or less what Kojève was hinting at when he spoke of the involution of modern (American) civilization towards the animal stage, that of a functional response and an automatic extraversion of all behaviours.

This is akin to the hypothesis that the human being is merely a premature ape. If he evolved towards a finished state, he would become an ape. It is the same with thought: if it evolved to a finished stage, it would become simian, being no longer anything but a parody, an ornamental variant of reality instead of being its parabolic mirror.

The weakness of many novels and films can be seen in the fact that one is forced to interpret them ironically to find any depth in them (*mise en abyme* is an effect of the same kind).

One is everywhere trapped between a literal and an ironic reading. A more or less conscious calculation that aims to disorientate any value judgement. It is particularly flagrant in the field of art, where this studied vagueness as to how a work is to be read has supplanted illusion and aesthetic judgement.

Deep down, however, it is reality itself that has become so banal and insignificant that it has induced us into an ironic reading. It has become so homogenized that it breaks off from itself into a parallel reality. It is out of nostalgia that we embed it in another order: in the face of this insignificance, we are forced to hypothesize a more subtle realm beyond, a dimension beyond our grasp. A critical masochism by which all the speculative arts have found success.

Tomorrow's Eve (Villiers de l'Isle-Adam). What invention, what richness of language! In those days they were not afraid of language. *We* are afraid of language since we have been told about the signifier and all that. The signifier has introduced terror into language. 'The Unconscious structured like a language' – nothing has wreaked such havoc as this kind of proposition.

There is a fantastic moment in *Tomorrow's Eve* (Villiers de l'Isle-Adam): the passage with Edison and his phonograph. Edison is complaining that this marvellous technique has been invented (by him) at a point when there is no longer anything worthwhile to record. 'If only I could have recorded Christ's sighs and the sound of the trumpets of Jericho!'[25] At bottom, however, he tells himself, those trumpets and the din they made were meaningful only to the actors in the drama, to those who heard them, and perhaps even just to the walls themselves, since they were the principal parties concerned.

Conclusion: if every sound has meaning only through the person affected by it, if every word exists only through the person to whom it speaks (we might add: if every image has meaning only through the person who sees it), everything that could have been stored and transferred by the phonograph since the dawn of time would merely be dead records, belonging as much to the past as the world they would have outlived.

This goes not just for the past, but for our project of storing all data. What value is there in this pile of cryogenized information? Doubtless, like the walls of Jericho, it is merely awaiting the trumpets that will bring it all down.

Can one envisage a femininity without women, in the same way as a finality without end?
It seems difficult for femininity to do without women.
Feminists, on the other hand, can very well do without femininity.

Who would be so strange under the sun as not to believe he is play-acting as long as he lives? Our sky itself, by the filter of clouds and atmosphere, play-acts light.

A British theatre company is recruiting a terminally ill patient. The prospective actors will have to guarantee they will be dead when the performances begin (in one or two months' time). One of the company's artistic directors explained that all the details of the role will be arranged in advance with the donor and his family. The presence of the corpse on stage 'is an important element of the show to help us dispel some of the mysteries surrounding death', he says.

In the face of extreme reality we are defenceless. But this is only a beginning. We are the aborigines, the anthropoids of the Virtual. In terms of world history, we are barely at the stage of the invention of fire and walking upright. Logically, it remains for us to be exploited and colonized by an even greater power.

The perfumes of the East were there to banish the miasmas of the corpse – the perfumes of the seventeenth century to banish the body's pestilences. Don't perfumes and make-up today still relate to this systematic cleansing of the corpse?

Waking out of a week-long coma, the first question was, Who is dead? Who is alive?

In this world, which is there without having asked my opinion, it ought rightly to be the case that death could do without me.

As with ignorance of the law, ignorance of desire is no excuse. But it is the same with desire as it is with power. Power has no need of me and I have no need of it. It doesn't miss me and I don't miss it.

I don't miss desire either, and it doesn't miss me. It is the era of wintry passions.

From the standpoint of misfortune there is every reason to transform the world. From the standpoint of Evil, there is no sense in wishing to do so. So every transformation of the world is done under the sign of misfortune.

Esoteric disaster.

Once there's no longer anything to exchange it for, suffering is value-less. It isn't even a punishment any longer; it's an accidental waste product, a pollution, and with it the same (insoluble) problem arises as with the elimination of waste and pollution.

What remains is to derive a moral advantage from suffering and misfortune.

'Where danger increases, there grows also that which saves,' says Hölderlin ('*Da, wo die Gefahr wächst, wächst das Rettende auch*').

It is the opposite today: '*Da, wo das Rettende wächst, wächst die Gefahr auch.*'

(In the excess of security lies extreme peril.)

Lichtenberg speaks somewhere of the 'freedom to think, without danger, for the truth'. By this he doubtless understands the right of speaking the truth without the danger of being thrown into prison by the monarch. But if, by removing a comma, we read, instead, the freedom to think 'without danger for the truth', things become much more interesting. For then it becomes a question of the capacity to think without imperilling truth (without risk of unveiling it). It is no longer the freedom of thought at odds with power, but the truth itself at odds with the freedom to think. The whole relationship between thought and truth is at issue. There is a profound difference between the thought that wants to make truth shine out and the thought that wants to keep it secret.

But you can also wish for both at the same time.

Eliminating all complications, all vexations. Without this protective obsession, no serenity. And without serenity, no lucidity.

To condemn torture as being in any case useless and unproductive is the most despicable of arguments. The implication is that if it were productive (in terms of information), it would be justified. The same with racism: to argue that there is no objective basis for racial differences is to imply that if there were such a basis, racism would be justified. Now, even if there were one, not only would it still be unjustified, but it is then that it would be absolutely unjustifiable.

When you reread a text you have just written, it is like a phantom limb; you have only the virtual, painful presence of it, like Ahab with his wooden leg.

Sometimes even, it is one's whole existence one perceives as a phantom limb, the nervous tickle being what remains.

There are cases when the original outdoes the simulacrum. For example, the sequined illumination of the Eiffel Tower is kitschier than its Las Vegas copy.

Not knowing who she is, she pursues others' identities. Then, tormented by an obscure remorse, she bares herself, exhibits herself, to the point of enjoying being unmasked. Which enables her to slip in everywhere on the pretext that she has nothing to hide. The real story is that she does not like herself, and does not like other people either. Hence this coldness and arrogance in the face of the veiled charm and diaphanous sweetness of the other (female) guest.

Nothing distinguishes a natural intelligence from something that can give off all the outward signs of it, and this includes faltering before the test of truth.

So one can give off all the outward signs of power, and this includes faltering before the test of strength. A simulation which produces, with just the requisite degree of derision, the image of an illusory normality.

'I discovered with amazement that my senses registered external reality, but my impulses never reached to my feelings. My feelings lived in a closed room, and I used them only to order and always premeditatedly. My reality was so profoundly split that I was no longer aware of it.

I existed on memories of feelings. I knew quite well how feelings should be reproduced, but my expression of them was never spontaneous. There was always a microsecond between my intuitive experience and its emotional expression . . .' (Ingmar Bergman).

It isn't the racism of the little people that poses a problem for the 'enlightened' minds. That can easily be explained by their inferior condition. It is the symptoms of racism among the 'higher' minds that present an insoluble contradiction since, in the humanist dream, genius is supposed to be associated with moral grandeur and just causes, in the way that imagination is supposed to be associated with power.

Nietzsche, Céline, Kazan, Riefenstahl (Alexandre Adler: 'the death of Leni Riefenstahl has brightened up my whole day'), Heidegger, Saul Bellow: all condemned by universal consciousness on the grounds of intelligence with evil.

Right thinking does not believe for a minute that genius can be rooted there of all places – in the intelligence of evil, in a form other than that of universal reason, in a form compatible with both the worst and the best, in something that might be said to be thought itself and which has ultimately nothing to do with 'critical' intelligence or, indeed, with political reason or morality.

At the other end of the Enlightenment spectrum there would be the Jews themselves who, while having greatly contributed to conceptualizing the universal, are, by their singularity, their exclusive form of worship and their profound incompatibility, the most striking denial of it. Which is entirely to their credit.

Has anyone ever shown an interest in how the dead live while they await the Last Judgement? In the contemplation of God, agreed. But they must surely have retained a memory of life and the living, a recollection of the world they have left behind. In that case, it must be hell not to be able to inform the living of this ultimate truth, the existence of the afterlife. By comparison, the silence from beyond the grave is much easier to bear for the living.

It is better to live eternally with a question than with an answer.

Every photographic image depends on the object's desire to be photographed. If it doesn't respond to the call, then let it sod off and take its chance elsewhere!

The rejection of domination is not limited to the rejection of being dominated, but implies also the rejection of dominating. If there were the same violence about that as about the refusal to be dominated, then even dreaming of revolution would have ended long ago.

Laziness is always accompanied by impatience, since it is out of laziness that we want to get to the end as quickly as possible. And haste is a form of premature ejaculation.

Hunting the wolf is an attempt to put an end to the idea that man is a wolf for other men. Already hunted for its natural ferocity, the wolf now finds itself condemned once and for all by the idea man has of himself, by the idea of his own ferocity.

'The age in which modernity was being invented and had not yet degenerated into a caricature of itself' (Canetti). A fine example of that degeneracy: the clone, which may be considered a caricature of the human at its highest evolutionary stage. At the apex and end of its possibilities, evolution retraces its own steps.

New form of redemption: debt, companies, crimes, scandals – as in the past with slaves, everything must be redeemed. Everything must be transfigured and at the same time, as in the sales, everything must go. Everywhere the tiniest waste product, the slightest desire is being given its hour of glory. But the historic prototype of redemption is that of work, which was granted such moral and historical value only so as to enable the slave to accede to it as a free man. In this way the curse fulfils itself.

Hopper says, 'If it can be said, then there's no point painting it.'
The reciprocal: 'If it can be painted, then there's no point talking about it.'

Biosphere 2. It was the first 'reality show' (experimental microcosm). A closed-circuit simulacrum of survival, but on the scale of the planet and the entire species. Since then, all the variants have followed the same model.

Accidents fade from memory as suddenly as they occur – only the body retains an imaginative sense of them. It is like a dream – a few seconds' very deep sleep on the motorway is enough to cause two absolutely different series to intersect: the universe in which you are present, but where nothing is happening, and the one in which the worst has happened, but in which you have no part.

Or the opposite: the universe in which you have no part or very little – that of existence – and the other in which you do have a part, but do so at the risk of your existence.

It is the critical intervention, by act or deed, that helps the system over the critical mass threshold – beyond which it would be in danger of entering the zone of extreme phenomena. The cunning of history, but a paradoxical cunning.

Of all activities, thinking is the one that requires the least energy. It is, then, the mental economy that best suits lymphatic or thwarted active types.

The most extraordinary thing in the Samarkand story is that it is said that death appeared 'surprised' by the behaviour of the soldier, who feels threatened when it signals to him. If death can be surprised, then it is human, endowed with human sensibility. It thereby becomes a partner, a collusive adversary. That is, doubtless, the only way to tame it: to make the human show through in what is the most inhuman of things.

So, when S. J. Lec says that it is not we who resist death, but it that resists us, and then ultimately gives in to us, he transforms the fateful event into a duel – death is not an end, it is a rival, a strange rival and one that has its weaknesses. This is what 'death throes' properly are: the rivalry between life and death.

The child that slumbers within us has become a confirmed insomniac. What is the point of growing up?

Some like to let their slips and parapraxes show through, to revel in their strange behaviour: they are absolutely set on having an Unconscious.

The spatio-temporal paradox according to Calvino: beyond a certain distance, there is no longer any possible response-time, especially when heavenly bodies are moving apart at the speed of light. The message then becomes absolute, definitive – it becomes *a truth*, irremediable, lost in the infinite, beyond reach.

This might be another version of the 'fateful': every act is irreversible, irrevocable; it cannot be corrected and is moving away from us luminously in the void. *Lost in translation.*

The problem is the same on the terrestrial scale. In a universe where individuals are moving apart irresistibly and things are, as it were, exceeding their escape velocity, messages have less and less time to come back. Or we are crushed like atoms in an irresistible contraction and, in that case, it is hyper-density that puts an end to any meaning or message. They can no longer escape.

Perhaps the two movements, the gravitational and the anti-gravitational, happen at the same time, and we are both further and further from each other, dispersed and disintegrated, and at the same time increasingly compacted, merged and forcibly integrated.

'The conscious decision to make a movement corresponds to an electrical event in the brain that happens 200 to 300 milliseconds after the beginning of the movement.'

'The experience of free determination of the will is nothing but an awareness of past events projected into the future' (Atlan).

This precession of the act over the will, of the movement over the decision is interesting. It is the very question of thought: is there, in thought itself, something that precedes thought? More broadly, it is the question of the world: is there, before the Big Bang, something that precedes the world?

This enquiry is essentially metaphysical. No point falling back on 'neuronal electricity'!

A three-dimensional shadow? A hologrammatic shadow? The Graz Tower: a building in the form of a shadow. This is, in itself, a misconception: what makes a shadow a shadow is the two dimensions (it is the same with the image).

Even the zebra's shadow has no stripes.

Ubu incarnate: we lag irreparably behind stupidity.

Where do you rate your pain on a sliding scale from 0 to 10?
0 = no pain, 10 = unbearable.
It's a bit like plucking daisy petals: he loves me, he loves me not . . . They are the petals of pain.

'I began to experience the pleasure of writing, and that pleasure has always been connected to some extent with the death of others, with death in general . . . This is the other side of the tapestry.

'I would say that writing, for me, is linked to death, perhaps essentially to the death of others. But this doesn't mean that writing might be said to be like murdering others and carrying out a definitively lethal act against them, against their existences, an act that would open up before me a free, sovereign space. Not at all. For me, to write is to be faced with the death of others, but it is essentially to be faced with others inasmuch as they are already dead. I speak, in a sense, over other people's corpses. I have to admit it, I postulate their deaths to some degree. I am in the situation of the anatomist carrying out an autopsy . . . I move around the body, I make an incision, I try to discover the organs and, in bringing those organs into the light, to show up the source of the lesion, the seat of the evil,[26] that something that characterized their lives and thinking, and which, in its negativity, ultimately organized all that they were . . . That poisonous heart of people and things – deep down, that is what I've always tried to bring out.

'At the same time, the only homage my writing can make to them is to discover both the truth of their lives and of their deaths, the morbid secret that explains how their lives led to their deaths. That point in the lives of others, where their lives veered dramatically towards death. There, for me, lies the possibility of writing' (Michel Foucault, interviewed by Claude Bonnefoy, 1966).[27]

This diabolic confession is a dramatic revelation. Suddenly, the hidden side of Foucault shows through, his accursed share, the 'other side of the tapestry'. Suddenly, the potential cruelty of a writing that presupposes the elimination of the Other, his putting-to-death, is revealed, of a 'surgical', anatomistic form of thought, akin to autopsy, and which, by his own admission, is out to find the 'seat of the evil' and is, then, very far removed from the rigorous investigation of truth effects and closer to a mental operator on the fringes of death. The weft of the tapestry is the intelligence of death, which, through writing, lends its energy to an inexorable analysis, to a rationality that is implacable, but simultaneously entirely ambiguous. Is there not an intelligence of Evil at work here? And doesn't critical intelligence itself (once again through the diabolic filter of writing) draw its force from this radical ellipsis of the Other, of the Living, and of the ends of Man in general? A marvellous denial, a marvellous defiance of the rational edifice of his *oeuvre*. A marvellous line of lucidity, of a secret lucidity that traces out a quite other intelligence, nearer to Evil than to an archaeology of knowledge.

This antagonistic truth, which has nothing to do with rational, epistemic, analytic construction, this lethal secret of writing is something the Foucauldians cannot cope with. They have already forgotten it, they never knew it. Erected by them into a discourse of truth, freighted with a force of objective elucidation, if not indeed a militant demand, Foucault cannot be suspected of this thinking with a scalpel that he speaks of, of this presumption of death (the death of others, which is worse). All this runs too violently counter to the idealist vision of thought that all the faithful, all the satellites and epigones have – all those who made the Great Analyst, the Grand Inquisitor, a tutelary (and feudal) reference. Which is why, no doubt, just as secretly, he despised them profoundly.

This Foucault is one we shall not forget in a hurry.

As a degree of stultification by medication set in, the idea came to me of a description of the present world that would have as a title that mysterious formula that was Canetti's mother's: the Phylogeny of Spinach, which she employed to stigmatize her son's useless metaphysical enquiry in an entirely corrupt, money-grubbing milieu. It would be a phenomenology of this world as though of a plant or proliferating legume, with simultaneous electrocution of all cultures (shock waves through all civilizations), etc.

The Lucidity Pact or the Intelligence of Evil could very well have been called – apophatically – *The Impact of Stupidity or the Unintelligence of Evil.*

Few world events are emblematic of a life, and form part of one's biography on the same footing as, and sometimes more profoundly than, personal events. I pride myself on having cut a single swathe from the Wall Street Crash of 1929 to the collapse of the Twin Towers in September 2001. From the one event to the other, there is something like a meteoric short-cut through an advancing globalism, following out its fateful course with an inexorable logic, beyond wars and 'historical' events, beyond the visible progress of societies. Something that must be described as monstrous unfolds in another dimension than that of the human efforts to control its course.

The perfect crime supposes perfect guilt.

Always veered more towards heresies, peasant revolts and millenarian uprisings than history and revolutions.

Everyone today, at the steering wheel or sitting in front of his screen, seeing all the world's events pass by as he pleases, can imagine himself the epicentre of universal consciousness, and see the world spirit pass before him (no need now to be Hegel to see the *Weltgeist* pass by on horseback – Napoleon).

The banalized individual has only to look at himself to see the *Weltgeist* pass by. The world spirit is fully achieved, not now in the form of the state or at the end of history, but in every monad that is now the centre of the universe.

'How is it that the centre is nowhere any longer, and we live on the periphery of an entirely visible world' (Baudouin de Bodinat).

The burying of the placenta: the homage done to what has not assumed the form of life, but accompanies life like the soul of a dead twin. A shapeless, but guardian shadow. Perhaps in the field of thought too there is this nourishing relic watching over us, this substance from before birth.

Lucidity as the mental equivalent of light in Hopper.
'I have never painted anything but light on a wall.'

All progress in the knowledge of man makes his identification more problematical. It is not a problem of complexity, but quite simply we do not know what he is. It is more complicated than complexity (Morin); it is of the order of duplicity. The more we advance, the more we realize the object is playing a double game, that it is developing in both directions at once, in the direction of good and of evil, and there is no possible synthesis, no transcendent solution to this fundamental divergence. Complexity can always resolve itself in a more complex equation, whereas this irresolvable divergence increases with every attempt we make to resolve it. The more we plumb man's depths along digital pathways, the more we dissect him genetically, the more impossible it will be to establish an image of him.

Even cross-disciplinarity will not master his duplicity. For his knowledge about himself is as ambivalent as he is himself. We shall never manage to identify this creature, whom self-knowledge alters in his essence, nor, therefore, shall we arrive at any future programming of the species.

During the American elections, an editorialist concluded his article with the words that his greatest fear was that one of the two candidates would be elected.

It was the only witty remark of the campaign.

It is, in fact, the opposite fear that haunts the political Unconscious: that no one will be elected, that the final decision will be impossible, that everything will finish in a dead heat, which is the inevitable end of any probabilist system. The real drama lies here, in this state of balance, a reflection of the inertia of a society and its indifference to itself.

At this point, the situation becomes random again, as is attested by the case in which a single elector in a state where the two parties are level can swing the state and thereby, if there is only a tiny difference at the national level, swing the whole election. A form of total, accidental power, which defies all political reason but is not without its funny side.

We have lost our shadows, not simply for lack of a light source, but for lack of a ground on which to shine. So, the trapeze artist doesn't need a net now, given the absence of ground to crash down on.

The fine parable of the man who has lost his key in the dark and looks for it under the street light because that's the only place there's any chance of finding it. It is more or less the same as Nietzsche's parable about objects and mirrors (if you focus on the mirror, you lose sight of the objects; if you focus on the objects, you lose sight of the mirror). You can't have both at the same time. The difference is that, in the story of the mirrors, the objects are in the place where you are looking, but are simply substituted by the surface that necessarily reflects them, whereas in the story of the key, the object is being sought not where it is, but where it would be found if it were (though it isn't).

In the first case, knowledge finds its way around in the play of representation. In the other, there is a disjunction: on the one hand, an area of light; on the other, darkness at the place where the key was lost. Is it better to be under the street lamp and fully in the light or elsewhere with the unfindable key?

Deep sleep is when you are asleep but not dreaming. Paradoxical sleep is the sleep in which you dream. So, only paradoxical thought is the thought in which you think. Is there, by analogy, a paradoxical state of death – a deep death and a death with dreams?

It is evil that speaks evil: evil can ventriloquize.

True immortality is the immortality of childhood and adolescence, where you never think you will have to die one day. The phantasm of immortality is merely the price paid for the certainty of dying. And it is ready to pay any price, including that of annihilating itself to achieve immortality.

In the past, some were prepared to lose their souls (their hope of eternal life) in a pact with the Devil to enjoy the privileges of mortal existence. Today we are ready to sacrifice any idea of a future immortality for a present corporeal immortality, a perpetual renewal in cloning. Immortality is no longer a metaphor. We want a *real* immortality, we want a technical incarnation of it here and now. This is the new pact with the Devil, sealed and signed in blood by the human race, which prefers to be cryogenized alive rather than await some hypothetical resurrection of bodies.

To manage to read one's own book without presumption of authorship, as though it were written by an unknown, of whom, in fact, one knows nothing. What image would you form of him? Would you want to know more? Is there a coherence – even an allusive coherence – in this set of fragments, which is precisely not even a set? Could you guess the books that have gone before and, if not reconstitute them, at least identify the lines of force – and weakness – as though working from a fragment of a hologram?

'A thin veneer of immediate reality is spread over natural and artificial matter, and whoever wishes to remain in the now, with the now, on the now, should please not break its tension film' (Nabokov).[28]

Wine changes to water, and water itself takes on a strangely insipid taste. Repugnance and tastelessness affect not only food, but the whole environment, events and speech. You become flavourless yourself, colourless and odourless – translucent, but lucid all the same.

Everything becomes a symptom – you become nosomaniacal. Is it from being lymphatic that you become lymphomic?

Rarefaction of the globules, sensory isolation, de-intensified zone – the ideal niche, protected by the repulsion that affects all your sensitive extremities, but not the mind which, for its part, enjoys exceptional freedom.

All secretions stop. Sweating, secretions, excretions, various pilosities – nothing oozes from the laundered body, the purified body, the body become self-cleansing. The skin on your face acquires a feminine smoothness and gentleness.

Alveolar self-defence. The Lion retreats into his cave, into the shadows, licking his paws and dreaming.

With time, something vulgar reappears: health, the signs of health. And a certain nostalgia for the state of grace, translucency and powerlessness of the illness.

God scoffs at (smiles at) those he sees denouncing the evils of which they are the cause.

Translator's Notes

1 The reference is to 'the wild bunch'.

2 Directed by Tonino Valerii and Sergio Leone. Lamar Cinema Corporation, Italy, 1973.

3 Fragment E476. Georg Christoph Lichtenberg (1742–1799) was a philosopher and natural scientist. He is generally credited with having introduced the aphorism into German literature.

4 The Collège de 'Pataphysique, which had ceased to publish the names of its members or involve itself in public manifestations some twenty-five years before, 'disocculted' itself in AD 2000 (year 127 of the 'pataphysical calendar).

5 'Transcendental satrap' is one of the highest ranks of the 'pataphysical order.

6 Luc Delahaye and Jean Baudrillard, *L'Autre*, trans. by Chris Turner (London: Phaidon, 1999).

7 Friedrich Nietzsche, *Daybreak: Thoughts on the Prejudices of Morality* (Cambridge: Cambridge University Press, 1982), p. 63.

8 There is a paradoxical play on the terms *humain* and *inhumain* here that has greater force in French, where the distinction between the (biologically) 'inhuman' and the (ethically) 'inhumane' is not made.

9 An early evening TV programme which uses latex puppets of leading political and media figures in a manner not dissimilar to the British *Spitting Image*.

10 Emilie Ruete, *Memoirs of an Arabian Princess from Zanzibar* (New York: M. Wiener, 1989). Originally published in German in 1886.

11 John Brunner, *Stand on Zanzibar* (London: Millennium, 1999; first published in 1968).

12 More precisely, at Borehamwood Studios in Hertfordshire where Kubrick's *2001: A Space Odyssey* was filmed. The documentary in question, *Opération Lune*, was directed by

William Karel for Point du Jour Production and Arte France. The English version bears the title *Dark Side of the Moon*.

13 Jorge Luis Borges, 'A Comment on August 23, 1944', in *Other Inquisitions* (London: Souvenir Press, 1973), pp. 135–6.

14 The Chiennes de Garde – 'watch bitches' rather than watch dogs – is a feminist group founded on 8 May 2000, concerned particularly to combat attacks on women in public life.

15 A reference to Descartes's phrase 'larvatus prodeo': 'I come forward masked (upon the stage of the world)'.

16 The fluorescent rabbit, known as Alba, was created at INRA in Paris. Each of its cells contained the gene for a fluorescent protein taken from the jellyfish *Aequorea victoria*. *Crepidula fornicata* is commonly known in English as the slipper limpet.

17 The reclusive, but extremely influential novelist and critic Maurice Blanchot (born 1927) died on 20 February 2003.

18 The emissary is Edward Rogers from Galactic Relay Center in the story 'Souvenir'. See Philip K. Dick, *Second Variety* (London: Millennium, 1999), p. 358.

19 Nietzsche, *Daybreak*, p. 141.

20 As many as 10,000 extra deaths, largely among old people, may have been caused by the heatwave that struck France in August 2002.

21 'Womankind – the everlasting irony in the life of the community – changes by intrigue the universal end of the government into a private end, transforms its universal activity into the work of some particular individual, and perverts the universal property of the state into a possession and ornament for the family' (*The Phenomenology of Spirit*, trans. A.V. Miller (Oxford: Oxford University Press, 1977), p. 288).

22 In English in the original. Baudrillard seems first to have encountered this phrase on the rear-view mirror of a hire car in the USA.

23 This phrase is an allusion to a line in Stéphane Mallarmé's 'Le Tombeau d'Edgar Poe': 'Tel qu'en lui-même enfin l'éternité le change.'

24 This passage first appears in Jean Baudrillard, *Simulacra and Simulation* (Ann Arbor: University of Michigan Press, 1994), p. 124. I have used the original translation by Sheila Faria Glaser here, though I have anglicized the spelling.

25 My translation from Villiers de l'Isle-Adam, *L'Ève future* (Paris: José Corti, 1987).

26 The French phrase here is '*le foyer du mal*', which might reasonably be translated as 'the seat of the disease (or disorder, malady, ailment, etc.)', but Baudrillard's commentary requires that *le mal* be rendered in its very broadest sense.

27 For the full text of the interview, see *Arts et Loisirs*, no. 38 (1966), pp. 8–9.

28 V. Nabokov, *Transparent Things* (1972) in *Novels, 1969–74* (New York: Library of America, 1996), p. 486.